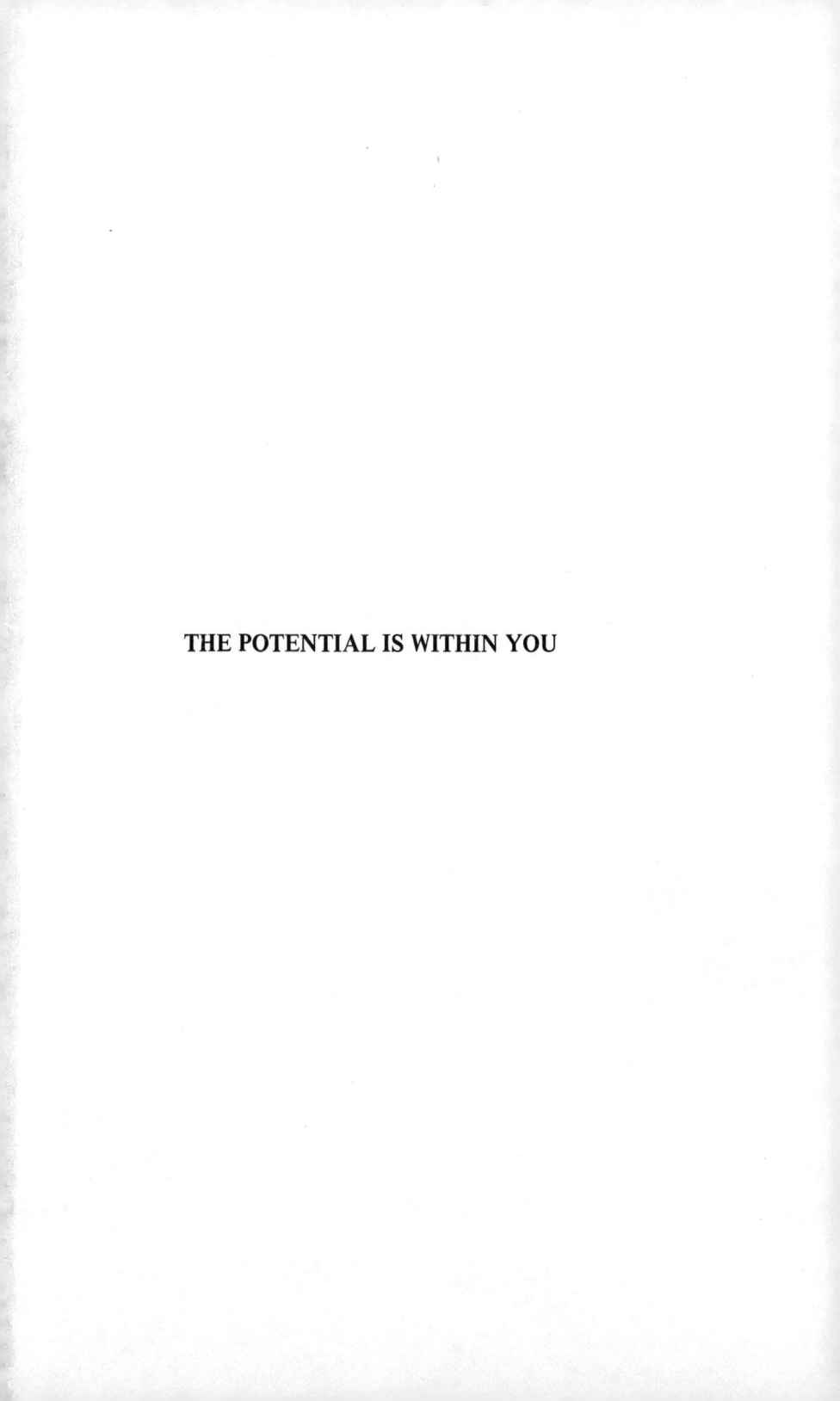

THE POTENTIAL IS WITHIN YOU

The POTENTIAL IS WITHIN YOU

Roy Eugene Davis

CSA PRESS, *Publishers*
Lakemont, Georgia
30552

Copyright © 1982 by Roy Eugene Davis

All rights reserved including the right of reproduction in whole or part, except for the purposes of review. Portions of material used appeared in Sciend of Mind magazine (May 1981) and New Thought magazine (Winter 1982). Published by CSA Press, religious literature department of Center For Spiritual Awareness, Post Office Box 7, Lake Rabun Road, Lakemont, Georgia 30552. Printed and manufactured in the United States of America.

Roy Eugene Davis began his studies in 1949 when he met the famed teacher, Paramahansa Yogananda, in Los Angeles, California. Since 1958 Mr. Davis has been speaking and writing on the principles of self-actualization and the realization of personal potential. He is the director of Center For Spiritual Awareness, editor-publisher of Truth Journal magazine, author of several books and a featured teacher at seminars and conferences throughout North America and Europe. His books are widely distributed in English, German, Portuguese and Japanese languages.

OTHER BOOKS BY THE AUTHOR

How to Use the Technique of Creative Imagination
Health, Healing & Total Living
Studies in Truth
Light and Philosophy of Yoga
The Teachings of the Masters of Perfection
Freedom Is Now
Conscious Immortality
With God, We Can
An Easy Guide to Meditation
Who Is the True Guru
Miracle Man of Japan
The Way of the Initiate
This Is Reality
Bhagavad Gita (commentary)
Secrets of Inner Power
Time, Space and Circumstance
The Path of Soul Realization

Contents

Preface	9
Chapter One Is A Life Without Limitations Possible?	15
Chapter Two Enlightenment is Our Natural Condition	33
Chapter Three Open Your Mind to Unlimited Good	47
Chapter Four Invite Life into Your World Through Creative Visualization	63
Chapter Five Meditation as a Conscious and Dynamic Experience	81
Chapter Six Keys to Emotional Harmony	99
Chapter Seven Regeneration and Radiant Living	115
Chapter Eight Experiencing Open and Supportive Relationships	127
Chapter Nine True and Lasting Prosperity for You	141
Chapter Ten The World is a Better Place Because of Who You Are	155

Preface

If the sharing of useful ways could work transformation of the human condition the planet would, by now, be enlightened. Both verbal and written information has been available for centuries relating to man's real nature and his innate potential. Only a few who receive the message have ears to hear, and fewer still among these attentive few can be motivated to action and actualization. Experience alone enables one to transmute information into personal realization. Unless what is known is actualized, made real through experience, information is just so much available data.

In these pages I have shared myself. I have also shared methods and procedures found useful by all successful people of the planet. How do I know this? Because I know myself and I know that nature is supported and continues because of inborn principles and laws. The inclination of nature, of life, is in the direction of awakening, unfoldment, creative expression and the fulfillment of destined ends. We have but to look about us in any natural setting to see this to be so. Nature is driven by a powerful force in the direction of function and growth. The soul of us, the real essence and being of us, is likewise driven in the direction of function and growth. We may attempt to deny the urge, but the urge will persist. We may, in our thousand little ways, try to remain unconscious of that which is obvious but, sooner or later, we will have to confront the truth. The *truth* is *that which is so* about *that which is*. A friend recently told me that her college professor advised her that this definition of *truth* was simplistic and not acceptable. The professor was either not aware of the truth or he was gently chiding his student as a teaching exercise. I am aware that many overly-simplistic actualization programs are today offered to the thousands of men and women who seek enlightenment. Some teachers of transformation processes are, themselves, not yet spiritually mature. This is not a critical evaluation or an effort to fault them for their sincere intent. God works in mysterious ways, His wonders to perform. Life works in unconventional ways in order to fulfill the evolutionary intention.

It may be simplistic of me to assert that we are in the dawning of the Age of Planetary Enlightenment. I admit to simplicity, and I have faith in God and the evolutionary process. This is not the place to expound upon the contest between the creationists and the evolutionists, whether the worlds were framed by an act of Divine Will or whether they were manifested through chemical mechanical chance-influence. I do not compromise when I state that both views are correct, because the divine and the material energy are involved. Yet, the material energies are extensions from the field of pure consciousness. Therefore, the intelligence driving the unfolding process of the worlds is grounded in the same field as is the energy which makes up the worlds. We can affirm that God is all in all, and we can affirm that the universe is a series of connected parts — all of which are formed of one primal essential substance. Our environment and all we perceive and relate to is energy-formed into whatever form or object we see, feel, taste, touch or smell. Therefore, never say that you do not know where God is. The energy flowing from the Oversoul, your own Larger True Self, is manifesting as all that you know about through your senses. The *you* who perceives is a specialized unit of a greater field of conscious awareness. One need not be a scientist or a minister to comprehend the essential workings of intelligent nature. One's vocation, if correct for the person, is a matter of destiny. All have the freedom to inquire and to discover. This book is for everyone, no matter the environmental background or the present mode of living. It is for you and it is for me, because we share a common sameness and a common ideal in the direction of final consumation.

Our origin is the same because we came from the field of pure consciousness. Our aspiration is the same because we are impelled by a common urge in the direction of knowledge and fulfillment. Our field of experience is the same because we share Planet Earth. What is true for you, in the final scene of this game of life, is true for me. I know a secret about you. I know that you are the same as I am, at the center, at the core, as the essence of life. Because I know this, I can share with you honestly as we explore our relationship with life together.

Roy Eugene Davis
Lakemont, Georgia, U.S.A.
January 5, 1982

How to Benefit From this Book

Read the entire text to become acquainted with the message and how it relates to you. Then, chapter by chapter, study the text and fill out the forms. It is by becoming involved with the principles that you will be able to experience needed inner changes and move in the direction of self-actualization and fulfillment. Use an extra notebook, if necessary, to write your goals and purposes.

"The one fact that I would cry from every housetop is this: the Good Life is waiting for us — here and now! . . . At this very moment we have the necessary techniques, both material and psychological, to create a full and satisfying life for everyone."
- *Burrus Frederic Skinner*

"I have been young, and now am old: yet have I not seen the righteous forsaken, nor his seed begging bread."
- *Psalms 37:25*

1
Is a Life Without Limitations Possible?

As we embark upon a useful program which can lead to change and transformation, we must ask deep within at a personal level if we really feel that change and transformation is possible. Let us ask of ourselves now: "Is a life without limitations possible?" Perhaps we cannot presently envision a life devoid of limitations. Perhaps we can envision only a life in which most limitations are no longer present as impossible challenges. Whatever our inner response, however we feel and believe, this is a starting point in the direction of greater fulfillment and possible complete self-actualization.

One may, if he is totally outwardly directed, affirm that the present environmental conditions are restrictive and even that forces beyond his control prevent creative expression. But, is this true? Why is it that, even during times of challenge, many men and women continue to function quite well and are able to set and achieve their goals with minimum effort? One may attempt to excuse his lack of success by claiming inadequate education, bad luck or a non-supportive environment during his formative years. There is plenty of evidence to prove that if a person is willing to decide, if he is willing to make a choice, lack of education and all of the other reasons one might give are but rationalizations for failure to face life and make intelligent use of present inborn talents and abilities.

The principles of thinking, action and achievement are available to any reasonable person and the principles, because they are laws of life, can be used by anyone who will learn to use them wisely. The laws of nature are exact; abide by them and we flourish, disregard them or misuse them and we fail. It is very important that we clearly understand an essential truth; we have a choice as to how we are going to live our lives and we can, if we so decide, make whatever needed inner or outer changes and work in harmony with the natural flow of nature. Life awakens, unfolds, moves in the direction of creative expression and, finally, experiences completion. When we are in harmony with nature's natural inclinations we, also, awaken, unfold, creatively express and experience completion. Lao-tse, in China thousands of years ago, shared a practical understanding: "The tree which fills the arms grew from the tiniest sprout. The journey of a thousand miles commenced with a single step." It does not matter if one is just beginning his personal journey in the direction of enlightenment and fulfillment; what matters is that once he begins, he is on the certain path to freedom. The joy of discovery and the satisfaction of accomplishment is just as real for one new on the path, as it is for one who had been living in harmony with the laws of mind and consciousness for many years.

Some who are inclined in the direction of fulfillment are mild in their intent. That is, they are content to see but a little improvement in their lives so they can experience a degree of freedom from pain and limitation. Others are more intense and purposeful. Perhaps, they are driven to put an end, completely, to limitation. Or, perhaps they seek power and influence. It may be that they are impelled by the purest motive of all, that of

Life Without Limitations

knowing the truth about life. It does not matter why one begins, for if he is rightly resolved he will soon experience change for the better and become possessed of understanding.

There is a supportive influence which runs through all of nature. This is why, no matter the chaos or temporary setback, life again stirs into activity and the process of growth begins anew. New life emerges from the old, new civilizations grow from the ashes of previous ones. When we clearly comprehend that there is a supportive influence in nature, we can make our plans with confidence because we have the very evolutionary power of the universe behind us when we flow with principles and processes which are innate to life.

When I stress the ideal of actualization and fulfillment, I do so in the understanding that it is not only our opportunity to experience actualization and fulfillment, it is our duty. Because we share our world with other people, the greater our freedom the more we can contribute in a useful way to the welfare of others. We are influenced, to a degree, by our environment and we influence, in turn, our environment because of our state of consciousness, mental attitude and general condition of health and wellness. The evolutionary trend today is in the direction of world uplift and harmony. Therefore, it is easier today than at any other time in history to make use of known principles and experience fulfillment.

A question is often asked: "If all reasonably intelligent people possess the inborn capacity to be free, healthy, functional and prosperous, why is it that so many in our world are not reflecting these conditions?" There are millions of people who do not know any better than to live as they do. There are millions more who know how to do better but they do not have the desire. Or, if they have the desire, they do not have the will to take positive steps in the direction of fulfillment. Because we are compassionate, our feelings go out to those less fortunate than ourselves and we wish for them a better existence. We can do our part to educate those who are open to such education and we can set the example by seeing to our own enlightenment and to our own freedom. As long as a person is reasonably conscious and has the will to excel, if he will choose to do so, he can unfold and experience the fulfillment of his innate potential. Some are born with good health and a healthy nervous system and, to them, the possibilities are almost without limit. For those who are not completely healthy and fully functional, they can, at least, extend themselves to their available limits. And, because the body is subject to change, we can, if we utilize known principles, invite the life-force to heal and transform the physical body and nervous system. If there are emotional conflicts, these can be resolved. If there are mental restrictions, these can be cleansed from the mental field. Let no person feel defeated as long as he has a degree of conscious awareness and a willingness to unfold and to move in the direction of completion.

Let us be clear that it is essential that one be willing to do whatever has to be done in the direction of change and transformation. We may have the will, but if we are not willing to experience change, will alone is not sufficient. When caught up in the flush of success we often anticipate change because we are anxious for the new unfoldment. When functioning at the level of working for an effect, without a true willingness to change, we experience frustration and inner conflict. We are sometimes afraid of change because we have grown accustomed to our present condition. We are sometimes afraid of the unknown and we may even become defensive when questioned or challenged.

**The Desire to Unfold
is an Innate Inclination**

Every living thing has the urge to be happy and free from pain or limitation. This is true from the plant kingdom to the human. Only a sick person is inclined in the direction of unconsciousness and death. Therefore, our will to live is an indication of our health and proof that we can unfold our innate potential. Human beings desire not only to be healthy and happy, but to be as conscious as possible in order to be aware of themselves and their world. There are some people who are reasonably happy and reasonably free in their personal world who are not as conscious as they could be. They are reasonably conscious but they are not expressing their full potential or they are, to a degree, limited by attitudes and beliefs which bind them to a known sphere of activity and relationships. To be happy and conscious one needs to be healthy and functional. Lack of health and inability to function is restrictive and prevents further growth. Man is naturally curious about himself, others and the world around him. This leads him to inquire and to ask questions, such as "Who am I? Why am I here? What is life all about?" This urge to inquire into the nature of things sets man apart from all other creatures. This urge to inquire into the nature of consciousness enables man to probe the spaces of the mental field and to come into a conscious realization of his real nature, his spiritual essence. Even a person who is not religious in the traditional sense, wonders about who he is and what lies ahead for him and others like him. A healthy person is endowed with a compassionate nature. We feel for other people, we feel for living things, we want to assist living beings and living creatures to fulfill their purpose. If our compassionate urge is influenced too much by intensity, we often try too hard to assist others, to the point of taking responsibility for their lives and, by so doing, deprive them of the opportunity of personal learning and growth.

With every step we take in the direction of self-actualization we also assume new responsibilities. We have to be sure that we are using our abilities wisely in relationship to the needs of others and in relationship to what is useful to our own health and fulfillment. The principles of thinking and action are available to all people, regardless of their personal drives and moral sense. However, if a person is attuned to the total process of self-actualization, he will become more mentally clear, more honest and more conscious of the need to function so that he contributes, not only to his own betterment, but to the betterment of all people whom his thoughts and actions influence. If we disregard the welfare of others, if we manipulate and control, if we work from a merely materialistic attitude, we will soon experience conflict and fall short of the ideal of satisfaction and fulfillment.

Remember, you were born with the innate urge to awaken, to unfold, to express and to experience fulfillment. Genius is resident within every person and has only to be released. Henry David Thoreau wrote, "I know of no more encouraging fact than the unquestionable ability of man to elevate his life by conscious endeavor." And Ralph Waldo Emerson wrote, "Everything in nature contains all the powers of nature. Everything is made of one hidden stuff." As children, we have read these thoughts and have perhaps forgotten them. Perhaps at an earlier age we were not able to grasp the significance of the words or the inspiration was soon forgotten because of the pressure of other matters. Haven't we all had moments when we inwardly knew of our true greatness? Haven't we all experienced these revealing occasions of direct perception of the truth about ourselves? In our quiet moments, when we are not relating to traditional thinking patterns, we are certain of our own immortality and of the promise life holds for us. We know that we did not begin at conception, and that we will not end when the body is no longer able to serve our needs. And, haven't we all had moments when we were possessed of inward vision, and we knew that our future could be altogether lovely if only we knew the keys to unlock the areas of the mind which seemed to be somewhat closed?

Life Without Limitations 21

**First Steps in the
Direction of Fulfillment**

Are we willing to release all thoughts, feelings and behavior patterns which are not useful to the realization of our chosen ends? Think in terms of what is useful and beneficial, in contrast to that which is not useful and beneficial. What will be our experience if we continue in the same pattern? What will be our experience, our reward, if we choose to change patterns of thinking, feeling and behavior? Here is a simple axiom which is as old as man's first conscious thought and as new as the moment: *If I do what I know I should do to succeed and accomplish my purposes, I cannot fail.* Repeat that sentence a few times until it becomes real to you. Use your imagination to inwardly picture how life can be, how satisfying the future will be when you function as the person you were meant to be. It may be that you have friends and close associates who do not share your dreams. If they can be encouraged to share your new outlook on life, share with them. If they are not interested, then keep your inner life private. If need be, change your relationships.

Think, feel and behave like an actualized person and you will soon be the person you want to be. You will call forth the talents, the abilities and the inner powers to unfold your innate potential. You see, the power of the universe is behind us because we are units of consciousness moving through time and space and relating to a universe which is energy. Learn to synchronize thinking, feeling and behavior because these areas of experience are interconnected. Think in terms of mind-feeling-body-behavior relationships. Function as a total unit to the best of your ability. Millions of people have worked hard at positive thinking and have failed. Others have stressed positive feeling while remaining negative in their mental outlook. Still others have learned to think and feel in a positive manner but they have not learned to function in a useful manner. Everything works together when we are truly functional; we think clearly, feel optimistic and relate intelligently. To be successful in our ventures, we have to feel worthy of success. Fear of success can defeat us no matter how hard we try to use the other principles. An attitude of being unworthy can close the door to fulfillment. There are many readers who will have to engage in deep self-examination and come to terms with patterns of thinking, feeling and behavior which have been long established in the deeper layers of mind and body. We are not doomed because of having remained in bondage to such patterns because we are superior to mind and body, and change can be experienced.

Have you forgotten how it was when you were younger and when discovery was thrilling? Have you allowed yourself to settle into a routine of living which is not useful? Have you done things you should not have done, and have you left undone those things which should have been taken care of? This is how it often is in human consciousness, but it is not the way it has to be from this moment forward, if you decide otherwise.

Cultivate the ideal attitudes, personal qualities and needed skills in relationships. Become an embodiment of the virtues. Read about successful people, inwardly relate to them, chart a course of responsible action and experience transformation. We can learn to adjust the mental attitude, we can cultivate ideal personal qualities, we can learn skills which will enable us to relate to other people and to life itself. Your thinking patterns will be changed beneficially as you assume responsibility for your mental attitude, interior conversations, mental pictures and verbal conversations. Let your attitudes and relationships reflect the highest ideal of which you are capable of contemplating. If you have not had the benefit of role models in your life, open the windows of your mind and find other people, in a personal relationship or through books and magazine articles, who seem to embody the ideals you wish to express. It is useful for us to actually see that other people are doing the things we want to do and that they have unfolded the potential within themselves.

Whenever you doubt, whenever you waver, turn within and be reminded that you are a unit of consciousness and that you possess all of the powers of nature within you. Do not allow yourself to be influenced by negative conversation, negative stories in the news media or by temporary lack of success. It is by remaining steadfast that we, in time, attain the victory and prove in our own lives the teachings of the actualized men and women who have preceded us.

Many of our patterns of thinking and behavior have been learned or acquired as a result of observing other people, or as a result of our learning to cope with our world. By observing other people in action, we might have decided, "That's the way people are. That's the way I must be." Relative to coping with life we are inclined, unless we know and do better, to function in whatever manner useful to our survival. We learn what works in our relationships and we perform accordingly. However, if we are relating to less than actualized people, we learn to relate in a less than optimum manner. We survive, we get along, but we do not unfold in a creative and dynamic manner. As we proceed with this program, we will more carefully examine methods and procedures useful to the purpose of eradicating self-defeating patterns.

Our values are reflected in our lives by the priorities we establish and by the condition of our environment. What is important to you? What is the condition of your personal and extended environment? Our personal world is an extension of our self-esteem and our feelings relative to what we feel we are worthy of experiencing. To paraphrase a commonly expressed axiom, "A person is known by the company he prefers to keep." The relationships we choose to maintain, the environment we choose to experience, the mode of life we choose to express and all that we do as part of our habitual pattern of living, is a reflection of our own state of mind and consciousness. Some people prefer supportive relationships, while other prefer relationships which result in conflict. Some people prefer order and harmony, others prefer disorder and disharmony. Some people prefer affluence, others prefer borderline poverty or just-getting-by. What we prefer is a reflection of the inner condition. If the outer world, our personal outer world, is not up to our standards we are free to change the inner attitudes and inner choices. No matter how successful we might become in the world we know through the senses, the material world, if we are not spiritually aware we are not ever going to experience true fulfillment. Our chosen form of worship is a personal matter and the religious tradition with which we feel led to affiliate is also a personal matter. Even if one is not inclined to affiliate with a traditional faith, there will yet be the inner need for coming to terms with life in some satisfying manner.

As we continue in this program, we will examine and take into consideration every aspect of life and living. To be self-actualized, we have to know who we are and we have to experience freedom in every aspect of life. As we unfold our innate abilities, we learn to appreciate all useful ways and all practices which have been beneficial to the human condition. Let us examine more closely the six areas to be considered and included in a balanced approach to true fulfillment.

1. *Spiritual Health* — One may be materially successful, yet spiritually impoverished. On the other hand, when one is spiritually healthy, enlightenment extends into every area of life. Where there is illness or restriction, we can almost be certain that there is need for spiritual awakening and deeper understanding of the laws of life. It is no accident that more in the healing

professions are supporting the approach that spirit, mind, body and relationships must be considered if complete healing is to be realized.

2. *Mental health and creativity* is vital to function. The mind is a creative medium, a tool we use to relate to our world and to the larger universe. We view our world through the mind we use. If patterns in the mental field are restrictive, ill health and inability to function freely is almost certain.

3. *Emotional harmony and serenity* is the ideal. Is it possible to experience emotional wellness? Yes, we can experience emotional wellness and live without conflicts once we are possessed of understanding and are willing to handle ourselves in relationship to events and circumstances, past, present and future.

4. *Physical health and vitality* is the ideal if we are to be free and functional in our present world. There is an innate drive in the direction of health and vitality, and when this is allowed to flow, we naturally experience a healthy condition.

5. *Open and supportive relationships* are the obvious reflection of spiritual, mental, emotional and physical health. It matters not how healthy a person appears to be, if he cannot enter into open and supportive relationships with other people and with his world, he has a problem at a deeper level.

6. *Economic freedom* is necessary for freedom of expression. Our wants and needs vary, but if we can easily do whatever we feel inclined to do, and if we are able to appropriate and utilize availale resources in an intelligent and honest manner, we are economically free. To prosper in all areas of life is the ideal.

What is Your Reality-World?

What you perceive, and believe to be true about what you perceive, is your reality-world. Your view of your world is determined by the picture in your own mind in relationship to your world. We are inclined to see what we assume is there, rather than to clearly perceive what is truly before us.

The understanding of a personal reality-world is as old as the *Veda*, the earliest known written records of personal revelation on the plant, and as current as today. William Glasser, M.D., perhaps best known for his book, *Reality Therapy*, recently wrote a book in consulation with William T. Powers on the theme of how living beings control what happens to them. The essence of the theory, as expressed by Dr. Glasser, is that beings have basic needs and they are inclined to sort out from their perceptions of their world those observations which will assist them to meet their needs. The next time you see an otherwise functional person behaving a little strange (from your viewpoint), realize that the person is perhaps attempting to meet his needs in the best way he knows. Unless we are very confused, we do not do things for which their is no reward of some kind.

A goal-directed person will see opportunity in almost any situation, while a person influenced by self-defeating patterns will see only that in his environment which will enable him to fail. We have all wondered why a person, with basic abilities and an attractive personality, will fail to see the obvious even when it is pointed out to him. Why is it, we ask, that some people will almost always grasp defeat from the very jaws of victory? Why is it that some people always seem to have bad luck, while the gods of fortune smile on their friends?

We can count our blessings, or we can complain about one circumstance after another. We can see solutions or we can see problems. We can experience answers, or we can remain confused by the questions. What we see in life is determined by our degree of conscious awareness and by what we want to see when we look or examine. It is true that in our larger environment,

Life Without Limitations

there are people whose conditions seem impossible to overcome. We have the poor, the ill, the too young to know any better, and the too old or disabled to care anymore. Even an impoverished person, if possessed of the will to excel and enough courage to dream, can move from poverty to affluence. If we are reasonably intelligent, if we will assume responsibility, we do not have to accept restricting conditions, because the environment in which we live is subject to change. Our personal world, our reality-world is of our own determination.

If you can inwardly accept enlightenment as your right and as your experience, you will be soon enlightened. If you can inwardly accept mental health and creativity as your natural condition, you will soon be mentally functional. If you can accept emotional wellness and peace as the ideal, you will soon be emotionally stable. If you can accept physical health and vitality as natural, you will soon be healthy and vigorous. If you can accept supportive and caring relationships, you will soon be supported and truly loved. If you can accept economic freedom, you will soon be prosperous in whatever line of endeavor you choose to excel. It cannot be otherwise, because this is the way the mind works and this is the way the laws of life respond.

POINTS TO REMEMBER
1. The Laws of life can be used by anyone.
2. Be purposeful in your intent to unfold and express.
3. It is our opportunity and duty to be self-actualized.
4. Be willing to do whatever is required to allow change and transformation.
5. You were born with the innate urge to awaken, to unfold, to express and to experience fulfillment.
6. Think, feel and behave like an actualized person and you will soon be the person you want to be.
7. Cultivate the ideal attitudes, personal qualities and skills in relationships. Become an embodiment of the virtues.

All Things Are Possible
Personal Planning Form

Use this page (and extra paper if you require it) to write your fondest dreams for yourself and others. Be aware, as you do this, that the forces of the universe are behind you and flow through you and around you.

**Actualization
Guidelines**

Acknowledge the power that runs the universe. Acknowledge the truth that you are possessed of inborn potential. From this moment onward, acknowledge the special nature of yourself. Be established in self-esteem, self-respect, because you are here for a unique and special purpose. You are here to glorify the life of the universe. You are here to learn lessons, understand the world process and to fulfill your destiny in harmony with a larger life.

Accept the ideal for yourself that you are destined to experience a life without limitations or restrictions. Be resolved never to accept anything less than wholeness and fulfillment.

Something to contemplate and realize:

"I was born to express the fullness of life. I entered into this world to awaken from the dream of mortality and to fully utilize my inborn potential. With God's help I will do all I can to be fully conscious and functional. I am thankful for this opportunity."

Notes for Plans & Projects

"In all my lectures I have taught one doctrine — the infinitude of the private man, the ever-availability to every man of the divine presence within his own mind, from which presence he draws, at his need, inexhaustible power."
- Ralph Waldo Emerson

"Lead me from the unreal to the real; lead me from darkness to light; lead me from death to immortality."
- Brihadaranayaka Upanishad

2
Enlightenment is Our Natural Condition

Enlightenment for a person is natural because it is not created, it is realized. If enlightenment were a state to be created or caused, it would not be permanent once experienced. Since causes are superior to effects, if enlightenment were caused it would be inferior to the cause which produced it. At the core of your being you are already enlightened. You have been enlightened, you are enlightened, you will be enlightened forever. At the center of being, you are pure awareness. It is only when we are identified with mental patterns and emotional and physical situations that we forget our essential nature. It is possible to be so conscious that we are always aware, on all levels, without losing awareness of our changeless nature as a being.

An enlightened person does not know everything about the workings of the universe but such a person can, if he so desires, know by direct perception or attract necessary information. The universe is open to one who is enlightened. From a relative point of view it seems as though there are degrees of enlightenment because inner knowing is somewhat veiled or obscured by the conflicts in the mental field and emotional nature. Behind all of the conflict, remains that undisturbed knowing which is never modified or dimmed.

Unknowingness is temporary because every person will, sooner or later, awaken to the awareness of the truth of his being in relationship to the larger field of life. The very existence of one's yearning to know the truth about life is evidence of innate awareness. We would not desire full awareness if there were not that inner awareness to prompt complete knowing. The way to enlightenment is the way of awakening and there are things we can do to allow it to manifest. Yearning to know is a powerful and impelling force that will remove all barriers to knowing. There are practical things we can do, also. We can do the very best we can to insure health and function at all levels, and we can abide by the laws of natural living as these laws become known to us. We have all exclaimed, during a moment of discovery, "I wish I had known that before!" What is past is past; we can begin from the moment of discovery or insight and utilize our new information to full advantage. Systems, methods, procedures and ways vary, and are many. What is important is that we use methods, procedures and ways which are useful to our purposes and realize that they are but tools for our use. When a task is finished we put our tools away. When enlightenment is experienced, we automatically live in accord with the flow of nature and we spontaneously do what is correct and appropriate in all circumstances. To abide by rules and guidelines cannot cause enlightenment, but can assist us to prepare a healthy condition and a firm psychological foundation for actualized living.

**Your Inner Intelligence
is the True Teacher**

Innate to every being is that intelligence of life with which all living creatures are endowed. Plants and animals are endowed with innate intelligence which directs the course of their lives in the direction of intended fulfillment. In man, the intelligence can be more completely unveiled so that he can, if he is inclined, modify his behavior, change his environment and roam the region of the stars. He can also roam the inner spaces of his mind and explore the depths of consciousness itself.

Our inner intelligence causes us to search for answers, to seek solutions, to strive for mastery, to desire the companionship of those more enlightened than we and to excel as we were meant to excel. The guidelines for one on the enlightenment quest are few and simple. They are also universal and apply to men and women everywhere who yearn to awaken and experience fulfillment.

1. *Inner and Outer Purity* — When one leads a pure life he rids himself of all that might contaminate or interfere with his highest aims and purposes. The removal of inner and outer restrictions can be the initial step for one on the path to self-knowledge and freedom of expression. We shall handle the details of arranging conditions so that purity is assured as we proceed through the following chapters.

2. *Intentional Self-Discipline* — Once we are possessed of a degree of understanding, it is up to us to decide to take positive action in whatever area of life that needs to be examined and handled. It is a matter of our doing what we know we must do, and of avoiding that which is not useful to our higher purposes. We can discipline ourselves so that we make wise use of time, energy and available working tools. We can train ourselves to clear unwanted patterns from the mental field. We can choose to be emotionally well. We can agree to live in harmony with nature and to be open to life's inclination in the direction of creative expression and fulfillment. We can do what we need to do if we choose to make a decision and move into a more enlightened and actualized life-experience.

3. *Careful Examination of the Laws of Life* — Many people are wasting time and energy because they have not learned the basic principles which can contribute to function and success. We have information, in books and through other sources, which has been shared by those who have gone before us. What is essential is that we examine what is shared and then make it our own through personal experience.

4. *Surrender of the Ego-sense* — The ego-sense is the false sense of being. We think, "I exist as a separate entity." This is error because we are units of a larger field of consciousness. This basic error in perception is at the root of most of the problems we have. As we live, as we experience, as we learn, we awaken to the awareness of a larger life and to the realization that we are but waves on an ocean of cosmic consciousness. As we set our goals and chart our course through life, it is well for us to ask, "What does the larger life want to do through and as this smaller expression of itself?" As we do this, we are able to expand our awareness and view life from a more useful angle; we are able to feel that we are participants in a drama which is vital and universal. It is then easier to nourish and support our brothers and sisters on Planet Earth and to nourish the planet itself with our involvements.

To aspire unto self-realization and enlightenment is the most unselfish thing a person can do, because the greater one's awareness of the life process, the more useful he is to the health of the human society and the evolutionary trend of nature. An enlightened person is supremely useful and supportive to all that is good.

Seven Levels of Awareness and Steps to Attainment

Seven levels of awareness are common to all who share the human condition. Seldom are we stable at one level, because we usually live from all levels simultaneously with an emphasis upon one or two levels as our usual pattern.

1. When one feels himself to be a physical body, that he was born and he will die and be no more, he is operating from the first level. Here, he thinks of himself as a material being, subject to the laws of the material universe. At this level a person might be intelligent, functional, a credit to the human race in all ways, but be unaware of his true nature as a spiritual being and unaware of his higher potential. Less conscious persons at this level of awareness may even be crude, cruel and extremely self-serving in their survival methods and in their personal relationships. After all, if we are mere bodies living on earth for a brief duration of time, why not get what we can and ignore the best interests of others? Thankfully, man's innate compassionate nature results in the majority of the human race having an attitude of concern for others.

2. From the first level, one awakens to a degree and begins to sense that there is more to his world than meets his casual conditioned gaze. He begins to remove himself from his reality-world attitude and is able to dimly glimpse something more real in the world he inhabits. He thinks that there may be something, after all, to this business of regulating thoughts, feelings and behavior. He begins to investigate the subtle side of nature, and learns of the existence of fine forces and energies which can be understood and directed for personal betterment.

3. Further awakening results in a person being able to more clearly comprehend the nature of the mind he uses, and he learns to use it with intention to serve his more enlightened purposes. The natural unfoldment at this level is that one becomes more comfortable in his relationship with the larger field of consciousness, and realizes that he is beginning to mature into a more cosmic being. His faculty of intelligence becomes more keen and his powers of intuition naturally become more prominent. By wisely using his keen powers of intelli-

gence he is able to discern solutions to problems. By using his powers of intuition, he is able to know things just by knowing and, perhaps, later find valid support for his extrasensory ability to know.

4. The next natural unfoldment is experienced when a person comes to the inner realization that he is, indeed, superior to mind and body and, therefore, must be more than a material being. This is the level of self-realization; realization of the true essence or beingness. Many falsely assume that when they understand their personality-drives they are enlightened or self-realized. They may be partially knowledgable but they are far from being truly enlightened. With self-realization there arises a natural sense of immortality, fear of death recedes and a person thinks more in terms of long-range goals and about a higher purpose.

5. By examining the nature of life and consciousness with keen intellectual and intuitive abilities, one is able to clearly comprehend the nature of the universe as a living organism. One is able to discern the rhythm and dance of life. Firmly established at this level of awareness, a person is a true citizen of the universe and all of his thoughts, feelings and involvements are only benevolent.

6/7. Beyond the fifth level we move into the realm of non-material qualities, and our greater range of perception and experience is in the field of consciousness which is not accessible to anyone not aware enough to experience it.

Some readers may not feel inclined to more closely examine the preceding information at this time. It may be that their pressing needs require the application of principles and procedures which can put an end to current difficulties, and enable them to reorganize their lives in an existing situation. It is my hope, that by providing information relative to man's total being, all readers will be served, each taking what he needs most urgently to begin the process of actualization and growth.

Enlightenment

While we can benefit from the support and encouragement provided by others in a group environment such as motivation seminars, awareness workshops, inspirational lectures, and wherever people gather to learn and improve their abilities, it is well to remember that we must see to our own unfoldment. Derive the utmost benefit from planned group programs, but avoid becoming dependent upon such gatherings. People who are busy actualizing the principles they learn do not have time for repeated non-useful gatherings. As long as you are motivated to excel, continue your involvement in such groups. If you can contribute to the usefulness of the group purpose, do so, as this will assist others and enable you to develop leadership skills. Carefully examine the usefulness of group participation. If you find yourself looking forward to the event as an opportunity to satisfy social needs, you are either not attending for the right reason, or there is nothing in the group gathering that you really need in order to get on with the process of growth.

Until we are fully functional, we all benefit from motivational opportunities. When we are open to new ideas we are quick to notice helpful articles in the newspapers and magazines we read. We can visit our local book source, subscribe to helpful periodicals, and turn the television or radio set to stations which carry helpful programs to meet many areas and levels of interest.

There is No Independent Universe, There is No Individual Person

Philosophers and scientists of the 20th-century are in agreement with their conclusions relative to the world in which we live and to which we relate. Scientific evidence supports intuitive insights to inform us that the material universe is formed of energy. Forms, things, are energy trapped into the observable patterns. Forms emerge in the sea of energy and, in time, energy is dispersed and flows back to the formless field of energy. Energy is constantly flowing, forming and then dissolving. The one certainty about our world is change. The speed of light, it is often assumed, is constant, but remains as a theory because of the sometimes irrational behavior light exhibits. The universe, from subtle to gross levels, is more and more being examined as one organic whole. There is an intelligence evident in the workings and flow of the universal order. Where is the heartbeat of the universe? Why is the universe? What is the purpose of life? Such questions are enough to give one pause and to offer an opportunity for insight to emerge. The world we know and experience, according to whether we view it as our personal reality-world or from a perspective which is more clear, is not independent of the source from which it emerged and by which it is nourished.

Is there such a being as an individual *you* or an individual *me*? We may think ourselves to be individual, but, are we? On the one hand, we are special because we are unique extensions of a greater life-source. On the other hand, we are but droplets raining down from a never ending process of life involvement. We are but units of awareness emerging for a duration on the screen of time and space to, one day, return to the source. When we are in tune with our real essence, we know we are immortal; when we are identified with the limited viewpoint of things, we feel doomed to extinction. The real inner knowing is the clue to who and what we are. We do not have to enter into a discussion about "new age views" or "current philosophical opinions to support present needs to cope", we can merely ask of ourselves, "What does my inner being say?"

Going With the Flow of Life

The more aware we are, the more we are caught up in the natural flow of life in the direction of unfoldment, creativity and fulfillment. There is a vast difference between the general pattern of experiences known to those who are open to life's evolutionary influence. Those who are not open to the flow are inclined to experience difficulty, hardship, problems and unexpected reverses. Aware people are inclined to experience harmony, opportunity, success and unplanned good fortune. Why is this? The reason is, the fewer the mental and emotional conflicts, the more open we are to guidance, inspiration and life's response to our wants and needs. When we are open to life's goodness we may not always know what is in the larger plan for us, but we are able to anticipate and expect the best. Life has ways of meeting us at our level of need in ways and, through channels, that we could not possibly envision. Make your plans, set your goals, be involved intelligently in useful projects and relationships — then, be open to the good that is even now moving in your direction and be ready to meet it when it surfaces in your life.

Different people have their own personal ways of expressing this activity of life in their affairs. One person might say, "Since I cleaned up my life, it seems that I am in the stream of grace." Another might affirm, "When I changed my thinking, I learned to see opportunity instead of impossible situations." However we express ourselves, once we are in tune with life and open to the flow, we begin to experience the nourishing and supportive influence of nature in all of our affairs.

To experience spiritual health, begin to have faith in what the enlightened teachers of the ages have said about man's relationship to the larger life. Begin to examine the nature of consciousness and acquire clear understanding, at least at the mental level, of how it is with you in relationship to the world in which you live. Then, learn to abide by the guidelines and procedures which can assure a life in harmony with natural laws and, in this way, come into your own personal experience. Correct understanding usually precedes actual realization.

We may understand the principles of life, but be unable to abide by them or utilize them completely. Practice, practice and more practice will make the difference.

Just remember, you are in partnership with a larger life and this larger life is your companion and your support in all that you do. The more we awaken to this understanding, the more evident is the activity of partnership and support.

POINTS TO REMEMBER
1. At the center of your being, you are pure awareness.
2. Your inner intelligence is the true teacher.
3. Examine again the guidelines on the enlightenment path.
4. Understand the several levels of soul awareness.
5. Benefit from all motivational opportunities.
6. Remember, you are in partnership with the larger life.

Goal Achievement Plans
SELF-REALIZATION

Goal or Final Purpose:

Affirm: *"I will complete my puposes and achieve my goals through intelligent involvement and God's help."*

Plans for Completion and/or Achievement:

Obstacles or Restrictions, if Any:

Solutions and Plans of Action:

Affirm: *"I will use these plans and experience solutions."*

Expected Benefits as a Result of Actualizing Plans:

Purposes Completed/Goals Achieved

Completed/Achieved _____ Date _____
Completed/Achieved _____ Date _____
Completed/Achieved _____ Date _____
Record short-term gains and achievements as well as long-term gains and achievements. Use extra blank pages in this book or another sheet of paper for more complete planning.

Actualization Guidelines

Become aware of your present level of soul awareness and endeavor to move to the next. Aspire unto the highest level of awareness which is possible. Aspire to live from the level of clear understanding. Take God as your companion in all that you do and in all relationships. Study the scriptures, discipline your senses, surrender ego-sense in order to awaken to your spiritual nature. Renounce all that is not useful and that is not in accord with the ideal manner of living. Associate with people who are living as you want to live. Cultivate the virtues. Embody all of the ideal characteristics. Trust life completely. Do not hesitate or delay in your resolve to move more and more in the direction of enlightened living.

Something to contemplate and realize:

"I consciously acknowledge that I am made in the image and likeness of God. I am possessed of all of the characteristics and qualities which are innate to the larger life. I see life as one organic whole and I live to the best of my ability as I know I should."

Notes for Plans & Projects

"The vivid force of his mind prevailed, and he fared forth far beyond the flaming ramparts of the heavens and traversed the boundless universe in thought and mind."
- Lucretius

"I beseech you therefore, brethren, by the mercies of God, that ye present your bodies a living sacrifice, holy, acceptable unto God, which is your reasonable service. And be not conformed to this world; but be ye transformed by the renewing of your mind, that ye may prove what is that good, and acceptable, and perfect, will of God."
- Romans 12:1, 2

3
Open Your Mind to Unlimited Good

The mind we use is a field of subtle energy through which we perceive our immediate environment. This mental field is a portion, a unit, of a larger field to which we refer as universal mind. Through the mind we use, we can work in harmony with the larger field of mind and, in this way, consciously and exactly experience a harmonious working relationship with the universe.

Consciously and intelligently used, our mind can assist us in the process of actualization and freedom. Unwisely used, the result is bondage. A point to remember is that the mind is our tool and we have the capacity to learn to use it wisely. There are levels of mental function, and order can be created and maintained between these levels. If the mental field is cluttered with rigid concepts, our perception of the world is screened through these concepts. A person will say, "I see the world this way!" Or, "Let me tell you how the world really is from my point of view!" We acknowledge that we are not the mind when we say, "I can't seem to control my mind." We affirm, "I'm going to change my mind about that situation." Within, at the core, is the being, the unit of awareness which observes mental activity and which has the capacity to use the mind intelligently.

We know people who, so it seems, were born bright

and intelligent. We also know those who, so it seems, were born dull and lacking in intelligence. We can recall moments of brightness and we can recall moments of confusion. We can recall occasions of high resolve and we can recall occassions of lethargy and, perhaps, despair. To order the processes of the mental field, it is helpful for one to assume an attitude of being competent. The mind, being a creative tool, is our servent.

**Four Aspects of
the Mental Field**

When we examine the nature of the mind, we usually become aware of the aspect used for thinking. At this level the mind is used for the purpose of observation, comparison, drawing conclusions and relating. Of course, there are deeper levels of the mental field of which most people are not aware. We know of the subconscious level, the storehouse of accumulated information, and we know of the deeper layers referred to as unconscious and deep unconscious. There are references given to areas of the mental field about which we know little, unless we are enlightened. Because we are aware of the thinking aspect of the mind, it is at this level we can work constructively almost immediately. We can, at this level, learn to organize our thinking patterns and to select thought patterns and ideas which are useful to our creative purposes. We can be selective when we are determined to intelligently utilize this mind we use. There is also an area of the mental field which is devoid of conditionings, and through which life's almost pure intention and influence flows. This is known as the superconscious level of the mental field. Superconsciousness is experienced during moments of transcendence or during occasions of deep, conscious, thoughtless meditation.

The feeling aspect of the mind enables us to desire and impels us to fulfill desire. After desire is satisfied, one experiences rest as a result of accomplishment. Desire guided by intelligence enables a person to achieve goals and fulfill destiny, while desire which is blind and impulsive can result in addictions and unsatisfying results. Because of the feeling aspect of the mind, one can become addicted, to a degree, to the satisfaction resulting from actualization experiences and neutralize the drives and desires which are harmful. Pleasure is not its own reward, but the pleasure experience resulting from accomplishment can be sufficiently rewarding to motivate a person, who is new on the path, to fulfillment and accomplishment. A few wins, a few short-term goals achieved, can be so satisfying that we are inspired to continue the process of goal achievement. Physical exercise may not be pleasurable when we first embark upon a planned program of improvement, but the resulting good feeling can be an incentive to continue. In time, the mind and body will actually begin to crave regular exercise. A mind, accustomed to temporary satisfaction as a result of sense-enjoyments, may resist the meditation process until the superior, longer-lasting pleasure of meditation is actually experienced.

Another aspect of the mental field is the faculty of intelligence, which enables us to examine a problem and discern the solution. There is mounting evidence that intellectual capacity can be increased, and that we are not limited by the intellectual capacity with which we were born. When the mental field is cleared and attuned to superconscious levels, intellect becomes sharper. After all, it is the being, the life unit which is really perceiving and discerning.

When we feel ourself to be a mind, or a personality with a mind, we then assume ourself to be an individual being. This is the ego-sense. When we say that a person has a large ego, we mean that he has an inflated opinion of himself. But, even a humble person, who considers himself to be alone against the world, or alone with others who are as he is, is functioning from ego-sense. When we expand awareness beyond the confines of the mental field, we realize that we are not restricted to a narrow point of focus. We realize that we are units of a larger field of consciousness.

Modifications of the Mental Field

We are all aware of the natural fluctuations which take place in the mental field. During the course of the average day, we experience occasions of being alert, occasions of tiredness and the duration of sleep. We also experience occasions of reverie, flights of fancy, and daydreams. One of the most definitive texts dealing with mental states and states of consciousness is *the Yoga Sutras* of Patanjali. In this treatise, various mental modifications are described. These are classified as; direct perception of that examined, indiscrimination, delusion, sleep and memory. When we see clearly that which is examined, we see, not based on our reality-world opinion, but what is so about what is examined. Or, we may fail to see clearly due to lack of discernment, and be in error relative to available data. If more unaware, we will be completely out of touch with present reality and be deluded. When we sleep, we withdraw attention from the environment and move in the direction of subconscious and deep unconscious levels. Even while sleeping, a degree of awareness is maintained because we remember, upon awakening, how well we slept. During dreams, we are often conscious enough to analyze the dream even while experiencing it. Memory is possible because of the recorded information retained at deeper levels of mind. By recalling these tracings of experience, we can vividly relive the past. Sometimes, we recall the past so clearly that we mistake the present for the past and react to a situation in the moment as though it were a previous situation.

At times, urges, drives and tendencies from deeper levels of the mind force their way to the surface levels

Open Your Mind 51

and cause us to behave in irrational ways. Once we recognize these drives and urges, we do not have to respond to them, no matter how strong their compelling influence. When these drives from deeper levels of the mind become pronounced we might exclaim, "I can't seem to help myself!" But, of course, we can if we are so determined. Occasionally, we read an item in the newspaper about a person who goes out of control and attributes his behavior to voices in his head. In some undeveloped cultures, these voices and their attendant urges are referred to as demons which inflict the unwary. Incantation, prayer and various rituals might be used to exorcise the demons and, when the process is successful, what has taken place is that the compelling tendencies have been either suppressed, eradicated or brought into an orderly relationship with other patterns and tendencies in the mental field.

**Practical Guidelines
for Wise Use of the Mind**

As we elect to choose sanity and orderly mental function, we learn to regulate conscious mental activities. We take our stand by inwardly acknowledging that we are able to master the mental processes, and we begin by training ourselves to think clearly and in an orderly manner. We learn to see clearly, to communicate fully and to handle ourselves in relationship to concepts and ideas. The ideal is to live in the awareness of the moment while drawing upon memory, handling present-time relationships, and planning without anxiety for the future. If we say that we do not want to think about the past or, about the future, we are usually admitting that we are afraid of handling memory and reluctant to take responsibility for ourselves relative to future unfoldments. There is no escape because, sooner or later, we will have to awaken and mature to the point where we can function realistically and in a rational manner.

Learn to be intentional when you speak. Even when involved in a relaxed social setting do not allow yourself to say things you do not believe, or that you do not want to be affirmed by the subconscious as being true. If you are goal-directed and orderly in your planning and achieving, carry this mental attitude with you all of the time. During a relaxed moment, even if inclined to do so, avoid saying such things as, "Life is a matter of luck. You win a few and you lose a few." Or, "I made a mistake on that last deal but, then, nobody is perfect." When relating with others, even if your companions share negative views, be sure that you do not inwardly agree. Monitor what you read, what you hear and what you think. Be discerning and do not allow yourself to become infected by the negative thoughts and opinions of other people.

What about the mental pictures we habitually entertain? Are they constructive or are they non-useful? For the most part, train yourself to envision achievement, unfoldment, success and prosperity. Remember, we are working in cooperation with a larger mental field, and this field is responsive to the thoughts we think and to the expectations we entertain. It costs us nothing but attention and discipline to order our thoughts and mental attitude. We do not have to tell anyone else of our inner work. All we have to do is to put the principles to the test and then see the results in our personal experience. If we are not willing to change our attitude, if we are not willing to regulate mental processes, we must be content to experience life as it has been unfolding. When I change inside, my world reflects the different image I retain for myself.

We are currently experiencing the results of prior thoughts, attitudes and expectations. This is referred to as fate, because it relates to cause and effect. Mental causes can be eradicated or weakened if we instill purposeful causes in the soil of the subconscious. We should not feel that we are doomed to be victims of past negative thoughts, desires, feelings or actions. There are many people who can testify to the experience of complete change and transformation as a result of having decided to assume responsibility for themselves in relationship to their world. If self-forgiveness is needed, this can be part of the change one makes. Even deepseated patterns and firmly established habits can be altered if we are willing to become decisive and responsible.

A frequent question, common to many on a self-improvement path, is "How do I know that I am on the right track?" Yes, we are wise to examine the motives for doing what we do. Are we driven by compulsions? Are we attempting to impress another? Do we seek fame and world recognition? Do we want money and things because we are afraid of being impoverished? Are we driving for success to prove to a living or dead parent or, another authority figure, that we can be successful? When we allow ourselves the opportunity to become quiet, when we are not influenced by any memory of the past or any present relationship, we are more inclined to be self-honest and to think in terms of what is really important to us. At such times we may experience inner guidance and a sense of being in tune with destiny. We may feel, "I have come to do a certain thing and to do it well, for my own unfoldment and as a service to others." Many are of the opinion, and I am one among the many, that each conscious person has a special place in the universal scheme. When this is allowed to become the dominant influence in our lives, we are inclined to experience health, function and fulfillment with minimum effort. Even if great effort is sometimes required, we find that hidden strength supports us and that a larger field of intelligence cooperates with us because we are participating with something larger than the ego-I, the selfish-self.

There are other influences which cause mental fluctuations. Unless we are strong and goal-directed we may overly react in the face of temporary failure or disapointment and become depressed. It may be that we experience swings in moods and attitudes due to faulty nutritional habits, or because of changes in body chemistry. Learn to take advantage of times when you are naturally strong and positive, and learn not to react too much during occasions when tempted to become depressed. See to a program of total wellness so that all systems function in harmony.

Do all that you can to maintain a totally supportive personal environment. See that your grooming, dress, living environment and work environment reflects the ideal you want to embody. Reinforce your positive intentions in every way you can, until you are stable and inwardly balanced as a functional person. Plan your daily activities, allowing for occasions of unplanned creative involvement, so that you utilize your energy and time to the best advantage. Many highly motivated men and women actually waste a large percentage of their time and energy in non-productive activities. Upon examination, it may be discovered that only twenty or thirty percent of the effort we put forth is productive. One could easily learn to be productive almost all of the time or, use the extra time and energy for other worthwhile purposes. If you are driven by your compulsions you over-extend yourself or, you exhaust your nervous system and body. Find out why you are so driven and handle that challenge to health and function. Sometimes, the most creatively productive times we have are those when we are resting or involved in recreation pursuits. Physical activity is important, but let us not forget that our ability to achieve goals begins in the mind.

What you can picture in your mind, if it is in harmony with natural laws, can be externalized or experienced. If you want to be happy, see yourself as being happy. If you want to be healthy, see yourself as being healthy. If you want to be fulfilled in a personal relationship, see yourself fulfilled in an ideal relationship. If you want to be prosperous, see yourself being prosperous. The mental pictures you entertain are shared with the larger mind of the universe, and the universe will assist you in the direction of fulfillment if you will only believe.

It may be that you are involved in a team effort to complete a project or achieve a worthy goal. Be sure, then, that all members of the team understand the mental processes and work together for a common purpose. If no other person shares your dreams, you can share your dreams with the larger mind which will never let you down.

The three keys to certain fulfillment are *idealize, believe* and *achieve*. Dare to envision, to plan, to soar to the heights in your mental planning. You deserve the best in life, so do not settle for anything less. Believe that all things are possible when you are working in cooperation with the larger mind. Then, as night follows day, you will move steadily in the direction of your firmly held conceptions. You may not know how life is going to work things out. You may not know which doors are going to open. You may not know when insight will surface. Persist in idealizing, in believing, and fulfillment is certain.

We are inclined to move in the direction of important events we anticipate. It is known that people, who are old or ill, will hold onto the body until a special event has been celebrated. They will maintain function until a birthday is reached, until the children come home from school at vacation time or, until a holiday season. When they no longer have anything to anticipate, they die to this world. It may be that we have attained all of our material goals, but there are still goals relating to the mental, emotional and spiritual realms before us.

The Powerful Influence of Intentional Affirmations

We have an available tool which can enable us to regulate mental patterns, emotional states, body chemistry, and our relationship with events and circumstances. What is this tool which is such a powerful influence for good? It is the practice of intentional affirmation. We can talk ourselves into a positive frame of mind, or we can talk ourselves into a negative mental attitude. We can talk ourselves out of emotional depressions, or we can talk ourselves into unhappy moods. We can even instruct the systems and the organs of the body to function more efficiently. We can also talk ourselves into constructive action, or into useless involvements.

When using an affirmation, always make a statement in the present moment that you desire to be true. Affirm, for instance, "I am a conscious and creative person. I always use my talents and abilities in the most effective and result-producing manner." Or, "I am a happy emotionally stable person. I always handle my attitudes and feelings wisely in relationship to circumstances." In rare instances, a bold affirmative statement may be too much of a challenge for the subconscious to accept as true. It may be, that the difference between what seems to be and what is idealized is so great, that the subconscious level of mind cannot accept the affirmative statement. In this instance, modify the affirmation so that the subconscious resistance is gradually dissolved. One might affirm, "I am now, rapidly and by gradual degrees, moving into the conscious awareness of health, happiness, mental creativity and prosperity." You know your own mind better than anyone else. Take an approach that will meet you at your level of need and acceptance.

You may want to begin your day by looking in the bathroom mirror and stating, aloud, "I am looking forward to this day with enthusiasm! I feel good, I feel competent, I feel creative! I move through this day easily and appropriately. I am open to my unplanned good, and I flow with life in harmony with the larger mind in which I live, move and have my moment-to-moment expression." At any time during the day, when you need an assist, use affirmations in a constructive manner.

Affirmations, correctly used, will neutralize negative

patterns in the subconscious. But we are doing more than attempting to recondition the patterns in the subconscious. The ideal is to be so conscious in the use of affirmations, that we actually awaken to the realization of that which is affirmed. We do not have to struggle to attempt to make the subconscious level of mind believe our statements. When we, ourselves, live in the understanding that our affirmative statements are the result of our inner realizations, the subconscious patterns will be rearranged automatically. When we are compelled from the level of the subconscious, even in useful direction, we are still being driven through life. The higher way is to be so conscious, so aware, so appropriate, that we live out of the awareness of the moment and flow with life's unfoldments in a natural self-actualized manner.

Whatever process we use, the ideal is to learn to live with an attitude of expectancy at all times. Expectancy, without anxiety, is the ideal because where there is anxiety, there is fear of the unknown and there will be the resulting stress accumulation in the system. Expectancy and perfect faith is the way to conscious living. When we walk by faith, we live in the inner assurance that our good is already prepared for us and has only to unfold on the screen of time and space.

The mental field has no power of its own. In recent years, some authors have written books about mind power and how to use it. The real power is the power of the person who uses the mind, and the real person is a unit of infinite consciousness with unlimited powers. It is true, however, that we can exercise will power. That is, we can intend to reach goals and we can intend for life to be responsive. This is not the same as being strong willed based on selfish motivations. But, no matter how much we intend for a thing to happen, or for an event to unfold, unless we can inwardly accept it as possible we will be struggling with life. Often, the simple act of acceptance can open the very windows of heaven so that the blessings flow without measure. Are we willing to be healthy? Are we willing to be happy? Are we willing to prosper? Are we willing to be self-actualized? These are basic questions we must ask of ourselves. The answers are sometimes surprising and always revealing.

An Exercise for Daily Practice

To open the windows of the mind, do this. Sit daily in a quiet place and be still. Let the mental field become clear and the feeling nature devoid of emotions. Acknowledge the truth about yourself: "Consciousness is what I am. The mind I use is a portion of the larger mind of the universe." Realize that you think in harmony with this larger mental field. Feel good about this understanding and this relationship. Then, go about your daily routine anchored in this understanding.

You see, one of the major problems for many people is that they feel they are in a contest with externals, or with forces beyond their control. However, when we are possessed of correct understanding, we realize that there are no enemies or threats in the external world because we are working in harmony with a larger mind which can correct any situation, open all doors, and be responsive to our personal wants and needs.

Any challenge that we have is not with impossible circumstances. If we are lonely, it is not because there are no persons who would be more than willing to be our friend and companion. If we are poor, it is not because of a shortage of energy or money or because of government regulations or job layoffs. If we overly grieve, the fault is not the person's who left us. It is we who are responsible for coming to terms with our world and for making needed inner adjustments in attitude, feeling and thinking. Our near and distant future fulfillment extends from us and from no other source. We, alone, through the freedom of choice, determine our future. Environmental change does play a part in our lives, but the final decision relative to ourselves and our relationship to life is ours.

POINTS TO REMEMBER
1. Your mind is a portion of the larger mind of the universe.
2. Understand the four aspects of the mental field.
3. Understand the modifications of the mental field.
4. Regulate inner and outer conversations.
5. Do all you can to provide and, maintain, a supportive environment.
6. Idealize, believe and achieve.
7. Learn to use affirmations correctly and with benefit.
8. Open the windows of your mind to unlimited good.

Goal Achievement Plans
MENTAL CREATIVITY

Goal or Final Purpose:

Affirm: *"I will complete my puposes and achieve my goals through intelligent involvement and God's help."*

Plans for Completion and/or Achievement:

Obstacles or Restrictions, if Any:

Solutions and Plans of Action:

Affirm: *"I will use these plans and experience solutions."*

Expected Benefits as a Result of Actualizing Plans:

Purposes Completed/Goals Achieved

Completed/Achieved_____ Date_____
Completed/Achieved_____ Date_____
Completed/Achieved_____ Date_____
Record short-term gains and achievements as well as long-term gains and achievements. Use extra blank pages in this book or another sheet of paper for more complete planning.

Actualization Guidelines

From this moment, accept personal responsibility for your mental attitude, your desires and beliefs, and your inner and verbal conversations. Be fully aware that you are the master of the mind you use. Be fully aware that when you use your mind creatively and intelligently, you are in conscious partnership with universal mind. Do not blame the past or the present. Be resolved to make wise use of your mental abilities. Accept the truth that you are becoming more intelligent and more capable with each passing day. Be free of all conditioned attitudes and beliefs. Allow yourself to be transformed as your mental field is renewed daily.

Something to contemplate and realize:

"I realize that I am a spiritual being, with the ability to use my mind in harmony with universal mind. I will order my thoughts, make intelligent choices, and share my creative endeavors with my world. I will plan wisely, see through problems to solutions, and accept challenge as an opportunity to unfold and become more capable."

> "The imagination may be compared to Adam's dream — he awoke and found it truth."
> — *John Keats*

> "The primary imagination I hold to be the living power and prime agent of all human perception, and as a repetition in the finite mind of the eternal act of creation in the infinite I Am. . . . The secondary imagination dissolves, diffuses, dissipates, in order to re-create; or where this is rendered impossible, yet still at all events it struggles to idealize and to unify. It is essentially vital, even as all objects (as objects) are essentially fixed and dead."
> — *Samuel Taylor Coleridge*

4
Invite Life Into Your World Through Creative Visualization

An innate ability of man is the ability to use imagination to image, or mentally picture, whatever he desires. On the screen of inner mind, we can picture anything we want to imagine for the purpose of problem-solving, goal-setting, comparing alternative possibilities or just for the pure enjoyment of having the experience. Sometimes we find escape through our daydreams or flights of fancy. But, when imagination is regulated by intention, we possess a creative tool which makes seeming miracles possible.

When using imagination for creative purposes, it is essential that we assume responsibility for our imaginative acts. A self-actualized person can handle as much of the substance of this world as he will take responsibility for handling. If our capacity is small, our abilities will be likewise small. If our capacity is large, our abilities will unfold in equal proportion. When we are determined to be goal-directed, we then mobilize all of our inner forces for intentional purposes. People who are not self-actualized use imagination, but without intention. They are aware of random thoughts and pictures floating through the mind, but they seldom single out any specific picture with the intention of having it actualized, made real, in their experience.

Now and then a person will tell me, "I just can't image, I just can't form mental pictures." Yet, upon being asked what they did during a vacation, or during any other pleasurable interlude, they will be able to accurately describe, in minute detail, the places they visited, the foods they consumed, the wonderful experiences they had, They may not have learned how to clearly picture imaginative situations, but just the same, mental pictures run through the mind as they describe their vacation experiences.

When we dream, during occasions of sleep, mental pictures circulate in the mind and we are possessed of inner vision. When totally relaxed during occasions of reverie, mental pictures are inwardly observed. When we learn to control our mental pictures, consciously and with purpose, we are able to influence beneficial change in our lives and even in environmental affairs. Think about it, haven't you, after experiencing the fulfillment of a desire, been able to remember back to a time when you formulated the desire and wanted the experience? Haven't you been able to trace a connection between thoughts and their outer results? Perhaps you expected something to happen, and it happened. Perhaps you wished for an experience, and it was presented to you. Perhaps you were just open to your unplanned, but expected, good fortune and good fortune came to you in a way that you could not anticipate.

Try it on something simple if, in the beginning, the process is a novel one to you. Try it on a project that isn't too important, because if the project isn't too important you will find it easier to "make believe" without being overly concerned with the final results. That is, you will not have any fear about lack of results and, therefore, will not imagine failure instead of success. Perhaps there is a small object you would like to have in your home or office, a book, anything at all. Just inwardly see yourself in the possession of the object and then let the desire drop from the conscious level of thinking into the realm of the subconscious. Soon, in a matter of hours or days, that desire will be fulfilled even if you do nothing to fulfill it. You can be involved with other projects and, soon, the inner picture will externalize as you desired it.

Why does this process work so effortlessly and so faultlessly? Because we are in tune, through the mind we use, with the larger mind of the universe. When a desire is retained at the level of the subconscious it is shared with the subconscious of the larger mind and, through various useful agencies, the desire is fulfilled. Every practical desire carries, within itself, the seed of its fulfillment. By practical, I mean that the desire relates to that which is possible in the realm of time and space, in harmony with nature's laws.

When using these principles of cause and effect, we always want to be unselfish and to think in terms of the best interests of all persons concerned. We do not have the right to invade another person's mind and make his choices for him, unless we are in a position where that person has given permission or when we are already responsible for the wellbeing of that person. Even so, sooner or later, we will have to release that person to life and allow him the freedom to determine his own relationships. Never, in dealing with others, do we think in terms of manipulation for personal gain. Some people can be manipulated because they are not self-determined, but if we use these principles for selfish purposes, we are creating problems for ourselves.

**Creative Visualization:
the Specific Process**

Once you know what you want to experience, once you are clear in your intention, if you need to use the following process follow the easy steps suggested.

1. Sit upright, recline in a comfortable chair or lie down. Be sure you are comfortable and can relax, but avoid a situation which is conducive to ready sleep. Let the mental field become clear, let your feelings be settled.

Rest in the awareness that "All things are possible in relationship to the larger mind of life."

2. Inwardly image a scene that would imply the fulfillment of your just desire. In your mind's eye, see yourself experiencing the fruits of success or accomplishment with all of the tones of reality. Do not think, at this time, of how you are going to experience fulfillment. Just enjoy the experience of fulfillment.

3. Feel the final experience of fulfillment totally, with every sense alive. Feel the reality and the "nowness" of the experience. Do not analyze, examine, picture contrary possibilities or, in any way, interfere with the enjoyment of fulfillment.

4. If light sleep follows naturally, flow with the experience of fulfilling sleep. Or, enjoy the sense of fulfillment until it settles into the deeper levels of mind and feeling and you are able to emerge from the session feeling rested, happy and thankful.

If, as a result of natural ability, you are able to envision a goal as already achieved without having to go through the process just explained, then function from that level. Many people are so actualized, that they have a desire and, automatically, feel that success is assured.

Another useful time to practice this exercise is just before going to sleep at bedtime. When the body is relaxed and the mind turns inward, picture youself in the general pattern of life you consider the ideal for you and for those with whom you share yourself. Perhaps you will not always deal in specifics. Perhaps you will just see, in general terms, how wonderful life can be and, is, in your present state of consciousness. Seal these attitudes and convictions in the soil of the subconscious, and you will find useful change in your everyday experience.

If, when using the step-by-step procedure, you cannot control your attention well enough to concentrate upon the inner picturing process, call upon the power of verbal speech as reinforcement. In your imagination, have a friend, in whom you have confidence, stand before you and call you by name. Have that person say, "(Your name), I am so glad to see you now fulfilled and to see that your cherished dreams have come true!" You, then, inwardly respond with a statement, backed by feeling, indicating your acknowledgement of their recognition. You might inwardly say, "Thank you, (the person's name), I very much appreciate your acknowledgement of my present fulfilled condition." You see, what you are now doing is that you are using the power of speech to order your thoughts and to regulate your feeling and believing. The end result is what you want to achieve. Any inner process you can use to cause the experience of reality is useful.

Once you have experienced the process, you need not repeat it unless you later find yourself wavering and losing faith. When you are established in the inner conviction that your goal is as good as achieved, regardless of temporary outer conditions or circumstances, it is impossible for you not to see desired results.

If, after using the process, you are inspired to do any creative thing to assist yourself in the direction of fulfillment, do whatever you are led to do. If you do not know what to do, leave the results to life because the larger mind of the universe is responsive and knows how to complete the picture, even if you lack the knowledge to do anything in that direction. Be open to opportunity. Be open to guidance. Life may reach out to you to fulfill your dreams through channels you have not expected, or do not even know exist at present.

I have usually noticed that there are two major reasons why a person who knows the process will refrain from using it. One, he may be afraid to assume responsibility for his own thoughts and actions. Two, he may be afraid that he is, somehow, interfering with the process of nature. In the first instance, we have to become responsible sooner or later. In the latter instance, remember that we always use the process in harmony with natural law and that we never desire anything for ourselves, or for another, which is not useful to ultimate health and fulfillment.

Sometimes, when using this process, we experience that the windows of the mind are opened and we can see almost unlimited possibilities. Make wise choices and then be open to unlimited good. Perhaps, life has something better for you than you can imagine! Accept that possibility and be open to life's goodness. At other times, we are free of mental activity and we seem to actually acquire insight into the future. We seem to know what is certain to unfold and, before long, it does. When this happens we are using intuition, the ability to know just by knowing. Sometimes we pick up on trends, sometimes we become aware of deeper mental patterns which are causing future events, sometimes we are open to what is already coming to us in due course of time. In this latter instance we have precognitive perception, because we can even know about other people and about other influences that are completely new to us. Later, when our inner perceptions are actualized we say, "I knew this was going to happen just as it did. I had no proof, but here it is, just as I saw it before."

What to do Between Now and Fulfillment

We want to be fulfilled inwardly, even if outer conditions have yet to be changed. While awaiting for desires to be realized and for dreams to come true, we should be preparing ourselves to handle the responsibility that goes with the new condition which is certain to unfold. We want to be able to meet the condition, or the relationships, in a mature and responsible manner. We prepare ourselves by improving our skills, adding to our fund of knowledge and, in every way, making sure that we are equal to the situation into which we are projecting ourself. I have met men and women who honestly want to experience fulfillment in one or more areas of their life, but they are not presently actively doing anything to prepare themselves. We might say, "Maybe I'll have a break, maybe I'll experience luck or, good fortune." Yes, but what if the break comes and fortune smiles upon us and we are not able to be equal to the opportunity? So, prepare, plan, do all that can be done to be a healthy, functional, human being. Think, feel and act as though failure were impossible. If you have a deadline established for a project with which you are involved, maintain a steady program of accomplishment which, each day, finds you closer to achievement. Do anything you can to saturate your mind with information and evidence that you are unfolding and becoming actualized.

If you want to take a vacation trip, but it seems that it will be impossible to arrange the money or the free time to manage it, do what you can to prepare. First, in your mind's eye, see yourself already enjoying the planned vacation. Acquire travel brochures and look at the pictures, read the descriptions of the places and events, and imagine yourself there. Make your arrangements, months ahead if need be, and as you move in the direction of your deadline, all outer circumstances will easily fall into place. If you want to buy a piece of property and build a house, but lack the money to do so at the moment, go ahead and investigate possible land sites and draw your building plans. Get as close to completion as you can. As you do, creative ideas will emerge and opportunities will present themselves. Act as though success were a foregone conclusion. Be the person you can be, do the things you can do, the results will follow naturally.

When I write a book such as the one you now hold in your hands, I follow an already proven course of action. The idea emerges in my mind to do the book. With the idea, I also think of a title and the general outline for the contents. I even mentally see the jacket design and I have a clear idea of the number of pages it will take to complete the project. Costs of manufacture, retail pricing, advertising plans, and other necessary aspects of the project come to mind, and I see the project completed in my imagination before I begin to write the first chapter. Then, I begin. I estimate how many days it will take for me to type the manuscript, and I estimate how many pages will have to be written each day to meet my self-imposed deadline. I open myself to ideas as I write, and during the day when not writing. I have the jacket art done and a sample jacket made so I can place it on a book from my library shelf. This enables me to "see" the finished product before the actual typesetting and printing begins. I do everything to make the finished book real to all of my senses.

A similar procedure can be followed for almost any useful project in which we may feel led to engage. If we are a part of the creative process, we will have to do our part if everything else is going to be able to fall into place. If we have a useful creative idea, the evolutionary energies in nature will bring together the right people and the right circumstances to actualize that idea. Creative ideas are the most important because, without ideas, without dreams, nothing innovative or unusual occurs in our world. Cycles continue and events tend to flow in the direction in which they are inclined, unless modified by circumstances or interfered with by a creative intention. Energy-efficient houses do not grow by themselves; space vehicles are not materialized on the launching pad; all things available for man's convenience in our modern age were not provided when the worlds were framed. Man takes available resources and energies and, through creative imagination and practical application, molds his environment to suit his needs.

We have stressed before, the importance of not sharing creative ideas with people who are inclined to attempt to dull our enthusiasm or to tell us we are imprac-

Creative Visualization 71

tical or are wasting our time. Avoid mental poison at all costs. Pray in secret, dream in secret, visualize in secret, and let the results speak for themselves. "Better done than talked about," is one axiom. Another is, "Don't talk about it, show me." And, "Actions speak louder than words." Results are the important conclusion to any creative act.

Use this Process to Make Your Dreams More Real

I know of people who, when planning their future, make a "wish book" by obtaining a large notebook and, in it, writing their goals. They also write known obstacles to the achieving of these goals, as well as possible ways to remove every obstacle. In this book they write affirmations, as well as creative ideas to be acted upon. They go further, they add photographs and drawings of things they want or of anything that will assist them to make their dreams more real in their own consciousness. By doing these things, they clarify their thinking, open themselves to ideas, feed the mind and emotional nature with data to support their creative intentions, and come as close as they can to the achievement of their goals and to the fulfillment of their purposes. Photographs can be obtained from books and magazines, catalogs, brochures, from any available source. I know of people who, when working on a specific project, place a photograph or drawing of the thing they want or the project they want to complete near the bathroom mirror, on the kitchen refrigerator, on the desk or a convenient bulletin board. Whenever they see this picture it is transferred to their subconscious, deeper levels of mind accept it, and creative processes continue in the direction of manifestation.

It is not uncommon for us to decide, after working on a project, that it is not really worthwhile or, that we started on the project before our thoughts were settled.

No problem: just modify the plans or cancel them altogether. Remember, you are the master of the mind you use and you have total freedom to change directions and make new decisions. To live with a mistake in judgement is self-defeating. By making decisions we learn, through experience, to make correct decisions most of the time. Eventually, when we are fully self-actualized, we will automatically make correct decisions in all instances and in all circumstances.

A major decision for many people is that of knowing where to place their attention and how to live their life. Haven't you heard a friend say, "I'm reasonably happy but I don't feel that I'm doing what I was meant to do." If this your personal challenge, use the principles we have been sharing to find your right place in life. If you continue to explore various avenues and possibilities, you may stumble into your right place, the place of destiny. But, there is an easier way to come into a fulfilling relationship with life. Use the technique of creative visualization to inwardly see and feel yourself to be a complete person. When you experience inner fulfillment, even if external evidence is not yet apparant, the law is that internal influences must propel you into the ideal relationship with your world.

You may ask, "How can I feel fulfilled if I have no supporting evidence about me to verify the feeling?" Open the windows of your mind and understand that you are often made to feel good, bad or indifferent as a result of what happens in your environment. If your environmental conditions can result in a change of attitude and moods, it will work the other way, also. If you can cultivate the attitude and the mood desired, the reflection will manifest in your environment as events and circumstances in perfect correspondence. All power is innate. Power and influence is not external to ourselves once we understand the law.

It may be that your present situation in life is ideal for you, but you are merely restless or unrealistic. Finding your true place in life, the place where you can best serve and best function, is your own personal responsibility. The ideal is to render some useful service and unfold your innate potential in a vocation or an activity which is uplifting, supportive and beneficial to your world. Think in terms of service, think in terms of doing what needs to be done. When you really love the work you do and love people, you will experience incredible energy and an endless stream of creative ideas. You will be happier, healthier and increasingly functional as you flow with life in harmony with life's own purpose, which is the fulfillment of the evolutionary process.

As you read these ideas, motivate yourself to act on them. Become involved with the procedures and methods. You may experience immediate success, or you may experience a duration of seeming non-response. Be persistent and patient, realizing that inner changes are being made and, before long, you will see evidence of the usefulness of the principles you have used and the influences you have put into motion. Avoid the tendency to become preoccupied with yourself to the extent that you become self-centered. Train yourself to be open, expansive, trusting and responsive to life's guidance. Remember that you are in partnership with the intelligence of the universe in everything that you do. When you see to living the ideal life and cultivating the virtues, your happiness and true fulfillment is assured. Take inspiration from the words of Ralph Waldo Emerson, "What lies behind us and what lies before us are tiny matters compared to what lies within us."

POINTS TO REMEMBER
1. Be responsible for your imaginative acts.
2. Use the technique of creative visualization on simple projects first.
3. Review the four stages of the creative visualization process.
4. Do practical things to set and achieve your worthwhile goals.
5. Learn to be fulfilled regardless of temporary external conditions.

Goal Achievement Plans
CREATIVE VISUALIZATION

Goal or Final Purpose:

Affirm: *"I will complete my puposes and achieve my goals through intelligent involvement and God's help."*

Plans for Completion and/or Achievement:

Obstacles or Restrictions, if Any:

Solutions and Plans of Action:

Affirm: *"I will use these plans and experience solutions."*

Expected Benefits as a Result of Actualizing Plans:

Purposes Completed/Goals Achieved

Completed/Achieved_____ Date_____
Completed/Achieved_____ Date_____
Completed/Achieved_____ Date_____
Record short-term gains and achievements as well as long-term gains and achievements. Use extra blank pages in this book or another sheet of paper for more complete planning.

Actualization Guidelines

Come to terms with your needs and purposes. Do not shirk your personal responsibilities and duties. Be honest with yourself, realize your needs and meet them. Realize your goals and achieve them. You were born to be free. You were born to be functional. You were born to do useful things in this world. Only compulsive and selfish desire is binding. Desire to unfold, to express creatively and to experience total fulfillment is inborn and the natural inclination of each person. Use the technique of creative visualization correctly and with intention. Learn to master states of consciousness and to work easily with the substance of this world.

Something to contemplate and realize:

"I am the master of my mental pictures and of my feelings. I see through appearances to that which is real, to that which is possible, to that which is the ideal for me and others. My inborn intelligence guides me in all that I do as I open myself to a more conscious relationship with life."

Notes for Plans & Projects

Notes for Plans & Projects

Notes for Plans & Projects

"When you close your doors, and make darkness within, remember never to say that you are alone, for you are not alone, nay, God is within, and your genius is within. And what need have they of light to see what they are doing?"
- Epictetus

"Let a man be elevated by contemplation on the Supreme Reality which exists within himself. For the person who has conquered human nature as a result of divine contemplation of the spiritual nature, the inmost life is a friend; but for one who has not realized his true spiritual nature, the inmost life will seem to be an enemy. When one has overcome the tendencies of his human nature and has attained to the realm of self-mastery, he is anchored in the awareness of his True Nature amidst all duralities and is at peace."
- Bhagavad Gita

5
Meditation as a Conscious and Dynamic Process

Whether it be a small community or a large city in the United States or in another country, whenever my theme is about meditation the response is always enthusiastic. The reason for this is that people are seeking to become aware of their relationship with the larger life and meditation, correctly practiced, is a process which makes this possible.

Meditation is the process by which we are able to relax the body, unstress the nervous system, clear the mental field and experience our true nature as pure being. While certain mental procedures may be used in the early stages of the meditation experience, as we progress, we flow attention to deeper layers of consciousness and literally remove ourselves from mental involvement. This is why the process is often referred to as one which results in a transcendental experience; one transcends identification with physical and mental processes during the peak experience.

Correctly practiced, meditation is not auto-conditioning and is not related to any hypnotic procedure. Certain auto-conditioning and hypnotic practices may result in a degree of relaxation and mild success in regulating mental, emotional, and behavior patterns, but a person who is directed to self-actualization is motivated by the desire to become fully awake and truly self-determined as a conscious being.

Reasons Why We Should Meditate on a Regular Schedule

There are many useful benefits to be experienced as a result of the regular practice of conscious and dynamic meditation. Notice that I am placing importance upon being conscious, and upon the process being dynamic. Partial awareness and a passive meditation experience is not the ideal if full benefits are desired. To drop into a borderline unconscious condition is not useful to higher purposes. To remain passive and involved with surging mental processes is not the goal. The purpose of meditation is, ultimately, that we might consciously rest in the awareness of unrestricted being. A non-meditator might wonder, "Why do you want to sit there in a thoughtless condition, when there are so many beautiful thoughts to think and so many wonderful things to do?" We rest, during meditation, in full conscious awareness of being. The result is that we can then turn our attention to thinking and relating, with better understanding and with greater powers of perception. There are many benefits to be experienced as a result of regular meditation. I will comment on just a few such benefits.

1. Deep meditation is actually more restful to the nervous system and mind than ordinary sleep. Often, during ordinary sleep, there is mental activity and all tensions are not released from the nervous system. Millions of people meditate, not for the purpose of self-realization, but because their health advisor has encouraged them to do so for the purpose of deep relaxation and the release of accumulated stress. Stress is one of the most common causes of internal discomfort and physical illness. In controlled situations, it has been observed that meditators experience a lowering of high blood pressure, the brain wave patterns indicate conscious restful awareness, and the body consumes less oxygen, while the carbon dioxide levels are decreased. Meditation, for relaxation purposes, is a prelude to the

practice of creative visualization, and the initial phase for consciously regulating internal processes formerly believed to be beyond the range of conscious control. It is now evident that, with correct supervision, a person can alter internal conditions through visualization to the point where the healing forces can be encouraged to correct body functions which have not been normal. The reason for this is that the being, the real person, is superior to mental function and mental influence extends into the body. From a higher point of view, it would appear that the mental field and the physical body are actually contained within us, instead of we being contained within them.

2. The practice of meditation awakens dormant vital forces which not only contribute to the regulating of internal body functions, but also tend to neutralize the decay process in the body. The total relaxation and mental clearing resulting from deep meditation allows superconscious forces, soul influence, to infiltrate the mental field and physical body. In the course of ordinary living, the average person accumulates mental conflict, emotional pain and physical weakness. These are cleared to the degree that soul force can flow into deeper levels throughout the systems. Even the destructive mental-emotional drives and tendencies are inclined to be resisted, restrained and, finally, cleansed as a result of superconscious influences. We see, then, that conscious and dynamic meditation is much more than a half-sleep condition during which we relax for a duration!

3. Meditation awakens intuition, the natural capacity to know by knowing, and clears the intellectual faculty which makes possible our ability to discern solutions to problems and to see reality instead of a reality-world. In many people, intuition is suppressed except during random occasions of transcendence. Also, because of mental confusion and the resulting "cloud of unknowing" which often pervades the mind, not all people are possessed of keen powers of observation and discernment.

As we meditate correctly, on a regular schedule, the mental field is increasingly cleansed and refined.

4. As a result of meditation, we notice that constructive urges, tendencies and motivations naturally emerge and become more dominant. We could say, to state the matter simply, "Meditators become nicer people." Their values change to the degree that they experience inner transformation. There is no possibility of a meditator, in the long run, ever misusing abilities which are awakened as a result of his practice. The reason for this is that, with increased awareness at the soul level, our moral sense is more unveiled and we are more inclined to think in terms of one humanity and one world.

5. Because meditation enables us to experience mental refinement, we are able to enjoy deep satisfaction at the center of being. This satisfaction is more fulfilling than any temporary satisfaction resulting from unwise use of sensory perceptions or harmful substances. Because one experiences deep, inner, satisfaction as a result of meditation, it is easier for a person to renounce dependencies upon relationships and activities which are not useful to the purpose of self-actualization. What one has not been able to accomplish through will power and firm resolve, one can accomplish as the result of correct meditation practice and experience.

6. Meditation prepares us for contemplation. At a certain stage of inward turning, the mental influences are no longer present and we are able to examine problems, be open to guidance, contemplate the meaning of life, and experience direct insight into that which is examined. This process of examining, which results in knowing, is termed "perfect contemplation."

7. Because we experience useful change as a result of meditation, we are certain to experience useful changes in our relationships with other people and with our total environment. It is also taught, by advanced teachers of meditation, that when we consciously rest in the awareness of our unconditioned nature, during meditation,

subtle influences emanate from us to beneficially influence our personal environment and extend into community and social consciousness. Because we all share a common and larger mental field, when we are able to function as clear beings, there is a natural constructive influence shared with the larger mental field. The "one mind common to all men" written of by Ralph Waldo Emerson, the New England transcendentalist, becomes healthier and more free of the conflicts and inertia which pervades it. During meditation, the brain wave patterns become synchronized, enabling the unfoldment and expression of the person's innate potential.

A regular schedule is recommended for the practice of meditation, because we become proficient with practice, and we are able to enjoy the satisfaction of completeness. If we are not regular in our practice, we may be inclined to accumulate stress in the systems and to accumulate mental and emotional conflicts without even realizing that the process is taking place. Twenty minutes twice a day is recommended for those newly beginning a meditation program. Surely, we can allot this brief interval for the practice of a procedure which will result in so many useful benefits, at so many levels.

Who Should Meditate?

Any person, in any walk of life, can only benefit from the practice of meditation. The purpose for meditation practice will be decided upon by the person himself; whether for relaxation, a prelude to creative visualization or healing, for the experience of pure awareness, or for deeper contemplation upon an agreed upon theme.

A business executive may meditate before he begins his day or, during an interlude at the office. A housewife may meditate in the morning after the family has left the house. It does not matter when we meditate, the important thing is to set a schedule and be regular in practice. Children can be taught to meditate rather easily and, they not only enjoy the process, but respond beautifully to it. When teaching children to meditate, be sure to stay with the basics and avoid any tendency to become involved (or involve them) with flights of fancy or illusory perceptions. Any reasonably rational person can meditate if he will follow the guidelines. If one emerges from a practice session feeling confused, he has not practiced correctly. If one emerges from the practice session with no memory of what transpired, he has not practiced consciously. Meditation is easy to practice. All that is required is the intention to follow the procedure, and to do so on a regular schedule. Some almost immediate results of meditation are: improved sense of wellbeing, improved outlook on life, an increase in energy, mental peace, emotional calmness, improved behavior, and better work and study habits.

Besides the regular schedule, if during the day you become confused or overstressed, retire to a private place for a few minutes and meditate. You will be refreshed, centered and better able to function.

Not all experience peak awareness, unrestricted awareness, while actually involved in the meditation process. They do, however, notice that during the day, when they are not planning to do so, they experience occassions of uplift, clarity in perception and a sense of harmony with their world.

A useful practice is for friends to gather for the purpose of group meditation. The ideal procedure is to come together, sit quietly, and disperse without discussing the experience. Group practice is useful for at least two reasons: the very intention to do it together results in a more meaningful experience for the individual; and new meditators, or those with personal challenges, are lifted by the influence of the others in the group who are experiencing positive response. I know of business organizations, where friends who are open to the idea, meditate on a regular schedule at the place of business be-

Meditation

fore starting the day's activities or, during a rest break. I know of many such groups which meet for a session once a week for the purpose of meditation. And, of course, it is common for staff members of a church to begin the day with meditation or to use the noon hour for this purpose.

How Do We Practice Conscious and Dynamic Meditation?

If you are new at the practice, you should begin with meditation for relaxation first and master this procedure. This process will be the basis for success in all other procedures to be used later. Here is how you do it:

1. Select a quiet place for practice. Approach the session with optimism. Realize that the inner you already knows how to meditate, and all you will be doing is giving yourself the opportunity to experience positive response.

2. Sit upright in a comfortable position, one in which you will not have to move or adjust your position for the duration of the practice. Restless movements will tend to interfere with concentration and deep relaxation.

3. Let your attention be aware of the natural pattern of breathing. Do not regulate the process, merely observe it. If you like, let your point of inner focus be directed to the space between the eyebrows. The reason for this will be explained later. Just sit quietly, be aware of inbreathing and outbreathing. Be aware of evidence of calmness as muscles relax, breathing slows, heart action slows and mental processes become more subtle. Just sit and be the observer of the process. As you become more relaxed, you will notice that you actually begin to enjoy the peace and serenity that results and that subconscious resistance to the process fades.

4. When you reach the peak experience for that session, when you feel calm, and as inwardly clear and stable as possible, rest in the experience for a duration.

Allow this clarity and calmness to saturate your mind, nervous system, emotional nature, and physical body. Feel that you are being cleansed and purified.

5. Emerge from the practice session feeling refreshed and go about your planned routine. Do not overly analyze the process. Merely practice on a regular schedule once or twice a day, for at least four to six weeks. Allow yourself time to notice beneficial changes.

Another useful procedure is this: just as you come out of meditation, inwardly remind yourself that you are a unique expression of the larger ocean of life, and that you are able to creatively use your mind, handle yourself in relationship to life, and to set and achieve useful goals. You will be better able to function as a self-actualized being as you continue to meditate correctly on a regular schedule.

If you want to use the technique of creative visualization, the time to do so is just before emerging from the practice of meditation. At this time, you are more calm, more mentally clear and in a better position to vividly picture and work in harmony with the creative forces in nature.

If you are in need of healing, of body or of affairs, use the process of creative visualization for this purpose. If you want to use creative visualization for another, or if you want to pray for another, do so after meditation just before terminating the process. When you do your creative work at this time, you are grounded in the power that nourishes the universe and your work will be much more effective than at any other time. In general, upon emerging from the meditation session, open your mind and being to the unlimited good of the universe and feel yourself in the flow of evolutionary forces. You may be amazed to see how much more clearly you perceive, and how many doors open to you as you relate to life from this expanded state of consciousness.

An Additional Tool for Concentration and Meditation

Do not become overly involved with techniques and methods. They can be useful, but the purpose of all techniques and methods is to use them as tools for final results. When you experience the results, put your tools aside. Sometimes, one has difficulty learning to concentrate. Concentration is understood, for our purpose, as single-pointed flowing of attention to the meditation focus. Do not think that concentration means to use undue effort. Concentration should take place naturally as we withdraw attention from externals, and from internal body and mind processes, and flow it to the idealized point of focus. Concentration is attained through patient practice. Renounce the mental battles and flow with the process. Anyone can use, as a concentration method, the time-tested procedure of watching the breathing pattern while inwardly listening to the sound of a meaningless word. A word with meaning is acceptable as long as it does not result in our straying from the purpose of practice. Use the word "one", if you like. Choose any word that suits you and inwardly listen to it (do not mentally repeat it) every time you exhale. This extra procedure can assist in keeping one fully involved with the process. Do not use a word that might cause you to become lulled in the direction of a passive state of mind or consciousness. If you are prone to be easily auto-conditioned and you use a word, such as "peace" you may be inclined to hypnotize yourself, through self-suggestion, into a peaceful condition but this is not the purpose of meditation. Meditation is practiced for the purpose of experiencing conscious awareness. Those who want to more fully condition the mental field through the incorrect use of affirmations are free to do so but, if unrestricted awareness is the goal, they will have to undo the conditionings sooner or later. Why add further conditioned patterns to a mind already overburdened with unwanted patterns? The way to freedom, the way to liberation of consciousness, is to decondition the mind and to function from the level of beingness.

Overcoming Obstacles to Meditation Success

A few obstacles to meditation success may include: restlessness, mental confusion, daydreaming, the tendency to sleep or to become unconscious, and the tendency to try too hard to succeed. If one will agree to practice, as instructed, all obstacles will soon be cleared. Even if the body is restless, sit still and refuse to move. Be the master of the body by making the decision to be in command of the situation. To get through confusion and the tendency to daydream, sit erect and be attentive to the technique. The mental field will, in time, become clear and concentration will prevail so that daydreaming is no longer a problem. To overcome the tendency to sleep or become unconscious, keep the attention flowing upward in the direction of the space between the eyebrows. Do not strain as you do this. Let the procedure be gentle. This upward flowing of attention will tend to bring body energies up from the lower extremities and to keep attention removed from subconscious and unconscious levels of the mental field.

Practice meditation and then give attention to the process of living. Avoid any tendency to sit around and talk about meditation and meditation experiences. Your experiences are personal and transformation will be sometimes rapid and sometimes gradual. Let inner changes be reflected in your improved function and enhanced condition of living. Do not believe that any person or any group has special secrets where meditation is concerned. True, some teaching traditions which are the result of research and experience, provide a broader base and more information. Always look for psychological health and productive living when you associate with individuals or groups who teach meditation procedures. As with all areas of your life, associate with experts and with intelligent and functional people. Some meditation teachings are offered within the framework of a religious tradition. If you feel attuned to the total presentation, this is the connection for you. Do not allow yourself to be in bondage to any person, or to any group which promises results only in exchange for obedience to their system, if the system contains unrealistic and cultish trappings.

Fear of the unknown sometimes presents a challenge to the beginning meditator. There is nothing to fear as we enter into a process which leads to greater understanding and improved health. When we meditate correctly, we are but allowing the attention to return to the source of life within us and we experience this consciously. Every day we sleep, and we are not afraid to go to sleep because we know that when we are rested, we will awaken. When we meditate, we turn within to consciously experience pure awareness and, when we have done so for an appropriate duration of time, we will return to external awareness easily and naturally.

A direct way to enter meditation, for many people, is to pray until the mind is clear and feelings are calmed. After prayer, when we relax in the silence, the meditation process will begin and continue through its cycle spontaneously. Some meditators prefer to use an affirmation as a prelude to the process. This is useful if one affirms correctly, that is, in a manner most useful for the real purpose of meditation. One can use a phrase which would imply the fulfillment of a meditation goal and repeat it with feeling and ever deepening concentration, until affirmation is forgotten and only the conscious awareness of that which was affirmed is realized. Any technique which enables us to relax and turn within consciously is useful, so long as the final result is experienced.

What About Various Inner Perceptions and Unusual Experiences?

Meditators sometimes report various inner perceptions and unexpected experiences for which they have not been prepared. As we relax and the energies are directed within to the brain centers, we might perceive an inner light. Random mental pictures are commonly perceived and these are not unlike dreams during twilight sleep. Sometimes we may inwardly see masses of light, the colors of which will vary. It may be that a white light is experienced as shining brilliantly in the midbrain, or that a blue light is perceived at the space between the eyebrows. Sometimes a blue light is perceived here, surrounded by a golden light. These light perceptions are natural due to the focused energies which flow upward along the spinal pathway and become concentrated in the brain. If our attention is more easily focused as a result of perceiving such lights, and if we remain alert and continue our meditation experience in a productive manner, the perception of such lights can be useful. One may be drawn into a degree of identification with light and find that this is, for them, a useful peak meditation experience. If you are one who does not easily see the inner lights, do not feel that you are not progressing in meditation. Your own inner intelligence will guide you when you are surrendered and alert to the changing inner processes.

Also, due to the upward flow of currents in the system, one may begin to perceive internal sounds of a subtle nature. There may be a variety of sounds or, perhaps, merely a steady sound occuring in the brain. Early sound perception often includes those sounds which are the result of various electrical activities taking place in the nervous system. More subtle sounds may emanate from the little known, but more subtle, energies circulating throughout the system. Whatever sound is heard, if your hear sounds, if you want to use the sound as an internal mantra as a focus for concentration, do so. Mantras are sounds used for the purpose of clearing the mental field, refining the nervous system and aiding concentration while meditating. You have your own mantra occuring within you, always. If you have been initiated into a mantra by a qualified meditation teacher, use that mantra and seek further instruction from that teacher or a teacher in that tradition. But, if you want to flow with the sound that you hear within as you become more relaxed, it is perfectly alright. Surrender to the sound. Merge in the sound. Yearn to know from whence the sound emanates. In this manner, your attention will be led through layers of the mental field to the source of all sound, the source of everything, the field of pure consciousness at the core of your being.

Be open to natural unfoldment in all areas of your life as you proceed with your meditation practices and other useful procedures. Avoid fanaticism and any tendency to lose your emotional balance. Is it true that some people awaken extraordinary abilities as a result of meditation and related procedures? Yes, of course, it is true. But, do not seek the unusual abilities as ends in themselves. See, first, to psychological health and a healthy relationship on all levels, and what is best for your continued growth will unfold in harmonious proportion. There are no real supernatural powers, because all abilities are natural to the soul once full awareness is experienced. What is easy for an awakened person to do may seem like a miracle to an unawakened person. There are subtle laws which can be utilized once we learn to apply them; once we have become responsible enough to know about them.

Every time you set a goal and visualize its completion, you are using soul ability. Every time you acknowledge the goodness of another person, and see that goodness actualized, you are using soul ability. Every time you discern clearly, perceive without error, and surrender to the flow of the universe, you are using soul ability.

If you are a beginning meditator, begin now to practice on a regular schedule. If you have been meditating for a while, examine your procedure to be sure that you are meditating correctly and that benefits are being experienced. An occasional question is, "If I am functioning well in all departments of my life, and am clear and aware, do I need to meditate?" Even those well advanced on the enlightenment path continue to meditate for the purpose of maintaining inward purity and to explore subtle aspects of consciousness. They also meditate to remain open to the flow of influences from the larger field of consciousness and to be conduits through which these influences can invade planetary consciousness. There are many men and women who seem unremarkable to casual gaze, who remain anchored in a conscious awareness of the truth of life. Their presence on the planet continues to shed light and provide nourishment to us all.

POINTS TO REMEMBER
1. Review the process of meditation to clearly understand it.
2. Resolve to practice on a regular schedule.
3. At any time during the day, when needed, be inwardly centered and calm.
4. Do not struggle with the meditation process, relax into it.
5. Banish all obstacles to meditation success.
6. Be an open channel through which superconscious influences benefit your world.

Goal Achievement Plans
MEDITATION

Goal or Final Purpose:

Affirm: *"I will complete my puposes and achieve my goals through intelligent involvement and God's help."*

Plans for Completion and/or Achievement:

Obstacles or Restrictions, if Any:

Solutions and Plans of Action:

Affirm: *"I will use these plans and experience solutions."*

Expected Benefits as a Result of Actualizing Plans:

Purposes Completed/Goals Achieved

Completed/Achieved_____ Date_____
Completed/Achieved_____ Date_____
Completed/Achieved_____ Date_____
Record short-term gains and achievements as well as long-term gains and achievements. Use extra blank pages in this book or another sheet of paper for more complete planning.

**Actualization
Guidelines**

Agree within yourself to meditate on a regular schedule for at least 90 days. Meditate without any anxiety for results. Just practice on schedule. Experience the cycle of meditation; inward turning, relaxation, peak experience, rest in the peak experience, and come out of meditation with an awareness of fulfillment and satisfaction. Reserve time after meditation for problem solving, goal setting, contemplation on a chosen theme or for praying for others. After meditation, be involved with useful relationships and creative projects. Perform your duties with full attention. In this way you will improve concentration and more greatly appreciate life and living. Your improved concentration and appreciation for life will also result in more satisfying meditation experiences.

Something to contemplate and realize:

"Daily I will enter into the silence of meditation to experience clear awareness and a conscious acknowledgement of my changeless nature. During meditation I will surrender to the process and allow my attention to flow through layers of mind to the center of being. After meditation, I will remain centered and relate to all areas of living from a spiritual point of view."

Notes for Plans & Projects

> "This one thing I do, forgetting those things which are behind, and reaching forth unto those things which are before, I press toward the mark."
> — Corinthians 3:13, 14

> "I have often thought that the best way to define a man's character would be to seek out the particular mental or moral attitude in which, when it came upon him, he felt himself most deeply and intensely active and alive. At such moments there is a voice inside which speaks and says, 'This is the real me!'"
> — William James

> "Right belief, right aims, right speech, right actions, right occupation, right endeavor, right mindfulness, right meditation."
> — the Buddha's Eightfold Path

6
Keys to Emotional Harmony

The seat of emotions is the being, the person using the mind and body. If the being were not present, mind would not be animated and the body would not be energized. Therefore, we are the root of emotions which manifest throughout mind and body systems. We have the ability to choose, if we will, to release conflict and to experience serenity and inner peace. It is important to realize that we have this choice, that we are responsible for our emotional life.

A person is inclined to be attracted to that which is useful to his purposes and to avoid that which is not useful. If we have limiting emotional problems, why are we retaining them? Why do we not clear the mental and emotional nature so that we can function without restriction? Deep down, inside of us, we have the answer to these questions. A person who is irrational, who is confused, may persist in destructive emotional behavior, but this is because such a person is non-life directed. For one reason or another, such a person wills to move in the direction of inability and uselessness. Most who read these pages will not be severely irrational, and will want to do all within their power to clear away any serious problems so that they can function more effectively.

Inner Conflict and the Resulting Ills

Even minor mental and emotional conflict interferes with natural function on many levels. Healing professions today recognize that many physical ailments often have a basis in mental and emotional conflict. Physical illness may be the result, not the cause, of mental and emotional problems. When mental and emotional conflicts are cleared, the healing energies are able to flow without interference and health of body is restored. The body is responsive to our real or imagined needs. If we enjoy a zest for life, we are inclined to function well on all levels. If we find life to be a severe challenge, we may unconsciously cause psychological problems and physical ailments so that we are incapable of functioning and, therefore, do not have to accept challenge. Or, perhaps we are not special in the eyes of others and we would like to attract more attention to ourselves. What better way than to have a problem that persists? Personal problems are marvelous ways to get attention. I have met a few people who are so lacking in will-to-live that they hold onto emotional and physical problems in order to keep disability checks flowing in on a regular schedule. If they recovered, if they became functional, they would have to produce like normal people.

A person who is emotionally immature may tend to magnify, enlarge in his own estimation, his problems. One may make a mistake and realize later that it was a mistake and decide never again to duplicate the error. This would be sufficient for a mature person. An immature person might carry a load of guilt until sufficient pain was experienced to allow him to feel alright about forgiving himself. If real suffering is felt to be necessary, the person might become ill, have an accident or sabotage a beautiful relationship, because he feels unworthy of having a good life while harboring guilt feelings. A person without goals may wallow in self-examination and fault-finding to avoid the creative process. Nancy Smith may have a secret desire for an intimate tryst with her girl friend's husband. She thinks it just awful to have such a thought. She feels guilty about the thought. She also feels guilty about feeling guilty because, after all, it was just a thought and no harm was done. Joe Smith might, in a flash of anger, wish his employer dead. After the anger subsides he might feel guilty about having had the thought. Thereafter, he goes out of his way to be nice to his employer, without telling him why he is being nice. Should the employer have an accident soon after Joe Smith has the death-wish for him, Joe might then feel extra guilty either because he feels his thoughts might have done the damage, or because it certainly was not nice to think such things about a person. We know, from experience, how complicated emotions can be, even when we understand the process. The purpose for this chapter is not to delve in-depth into abnormal or, even, normal psychology but to lend an assist to anyone wishing to experience peace of mind and emotional serenity.

We have friends who will admit to being lazy. We also have friends who will admit to being driven, as though by hidden compulsions, to forever be busy, to attain, to do, to produce, to prove themselves. What is important is that we understand ourselves and our relationships. What is important is that we acquire a clear understanding of our essential nature, the nature and workings of the mind, and guidelines to effective communication. A self-fulfilled person, one who is healthy, does not have insurmountable problems. A stress-free person is unlikely to have severe conflicts. The majority of our problems arise from the fact that we get off-center and forget who and what we are.

Calm analysis of an emotional problem may enable us to experience release. On the other hand, too much mental probing, without insight being acquired, may only cause us to become more confused. What is often needed is a change in attitude, a change in thinking patterns, a change in feeling, a change in behavior, and a change in how we relate to other people. If we cannot think our way out of a problem, perhaps we can act our way out by purposely experimenting, by altering moods and regulating behavior. There is much to be said about assuming a virtue even though it is not yet natural to us. There is much to be said about doing the right and appropriate thing even though we may not feel like doing it. With practice, almost anyone can regulate verbal expressions, body movements and relationships. We can cease from speaking, if we are about to say something out of line. We can stand and move in a controlled manner. We can commence and terminate relationships at will, according to how we deem ideal. One may be inclined to be mean, petty, assertive and resentful, but one does not have to dramatize these inclinations. Unwanted inclinations and tendencies can be transmuted into more useful drives. Non-productive behavior can be changed to useful behavior. We can change, if we are willing to assume the responsibility for changing. If we want to remain the victim of harmful habits, we can remain a victim. If we want to be free of such habits, we can be free. We have the ability to decide because the power of life itself resides within us.

A Simple Approach to Emotional Wellness

On two occasions, I have been invited to Japan to speak to members of a large organization, Seicho-No-Ie. The teaching emphasis of this movement, founded by Masaharu Taniguchi many years ago, is similar to that taught by many of our own New Thought groups. Ministers of this Japan based movement often counsel people who come for physical, psychological and spiritual help. Knowing that many physical problems have their roots in mental and emotional conflict, a very direct approach is initially made, and often it opens the doors to health. The one seeking help is reminded of the truth of his being, that he is a specialized unit of a larger field of consciousness and, therefore, does not have to have a problem of any kind. Insight dawns and harmony is restored on all levels. Perhaps, partial insight is not sufficient to meet the challenge. Next, the person is asked to feel good about himself and to feel that he is on friendly terms with all people in the universe, with all living creatures, and with the energies of nature. The ideal is: "I am now on friendly terms with a friendly and benevolent universe. I am so grateful, I am so happy." This change in attitude and realization is often enough to result in healing of even serious conditions.

When we realize that the "enemy" is not out-there, we are able to come into a harmonious relationship with our own inner processes and the world about us. Perhaps someone has injured you intentionally, or unknowingly, and you are resentful. What to do? Perhaps the matter can be cleared as a result of open and friendly communication. What if the feeling of resentment persists in you? How about praying for the welfare of the person? How about praying for self-forgiveness?

Once we realize that no external thing has power over us, we are in a position to be settled in understanding. A person may claim to be addicted to a habit, a behavior, a way of thinking and feeling. This is only so because it is being allowed. If we say, "I have this fixation!," we are affirming that we possess it. If we say, "I have this addiction!," we are affirming that we possess it. If we say that we are possessed by a fixation or an addiction, we are in error because fixations and addictions have no independent power to claim us. Alchohol cannot attack us, drugs cannot reach out and attach themselves to us, food doesn't lie in wait to pounce upon us, ideas and feelings are not entities with self-determinism. There is no power in any external condition, person, situation or thing that can invade our consciousness and enslave us.

An abnormal craving for food is almost always an indication of a psychological problem. Why is one driven to become obese and remain in this unhealthy condition? Excessive alcohol intake is evidence of a deeper psychological need; a desire to escape, to fail, to become unconscious and not have to confront challenge or, perhaps a convenient method for communicating with one's self. In the latter instance one may inwardly think, "I have no meaningful relationships to give me satisfaction, so I will cause a change in mood and generate different feelings by drinking." The problem in alcoholism is not the alcohol, it is the person. Heal the person and alcohol no longer represents a threat. The problem in drug use is not the drug, it is the person. Heal the person and drugs remain substances without attraction. Many excuses can be given for a person's destructive use of food, alcohol, drugs, automobiles and other substances and implements used to cause damage and interfere with the process of living. The need is always for individuals to get straight with themselves. Environmental influence is another excuse often used. "Everyone does it," some say. "My friends do it," others claim. It still comes back to the person and his own willingness to make wise choices.

A constructive step for many who are weak in the face of temptation is to remove themselves from the opportunity of being tempted. This may not remove the inner craving, but it will effectively prevent indulgence. Each time we resist a destructive impulse we become stronger. Eventually, the craving is eliminated altogether, especially if we redirect our energies into more healthful and productive lines of endeavor. Also, as we do our part to insure total health and vitality, and a balancing of all of our systems and inner processes, we feel better and are more inclined to continue in the direction of increased health and function.

Emotional Harmony 105

    Sometimes we hurt so bad we are rendered almost immobile. It may be that we were rejected in love, that we failed in a business venture, that someone close to us died. What one person handles easily, another person might experience as painful emotional upset. We have a choice in the matter of how we respond. We can hurt and become bitter and resentful. We can hurt and then get through the hurt and emerge a healthier, wiser person. We can understand the situation, why it occurred, and what we can do to relate to it without pain.

    It is natural to feel a sense of loss when someone close to us departs unexpectedly, or dies. Death seems such a final departure. Yet, even death can be understood because only the body dies, the person who functioned through that body still lives. If we overly grieve, our grief is for ourselves, not for the person who left because that person is still moving on to new and varied perceptions and experiences. How do we know this to be so? Because enlightened teachers tell us. Also, our innate understanding informs us that we are forever and forever, even though the body itself is subject to time and events. Perhaps, after a loved one has died, we feel grief because we did not do all we could for them while we had the chance. It may be that differences were unresolved before they made their transition and we feel bad about this situation. We can pray for the welfare of that person and we can pray until we feel an inner assurance that all is well. This is excellent therapy, always, to pray for others and to clear our thinking and our feeling in relationship to them.

    Perhaps we said something or, did something, to another person that was unkind and we can no longer make it up to them or obtain their forgiveness. Perhaps someone hurt us and the memory is as vivid and as painful as the moment the incident first occurred. A wise person is able to see through all happenings and make inner adjustments in a mature manner. But, we are not always so wise in our learning stages. We may know better, but find it next to impossible to do any better. Somehow, the emotional hurt must be drained from the feeling nature. The following process can often be useful.

Use the technique of creative visualization and relive the incident or, chain of incidents, with vivid clarity and feeling, and probe for insight and understanding. If this is not forthcoming, relive the scenes and run them through the mind, with feeling, as you would have liked for them to have taken place. Do not play mind-games and indulge in fantasy and illusion. Be perfectly aware that you are doing this only for the purpose of being able to experience an ideal situation which can result in the neutralizing of the pain stored in the emotional energy-mass. You will, with practice, be able to retain the memory of what really happened but, without the heavy pain-memory-response which once burdened you. This process of revision can be useful in many instances to cleanse unwanted patterns from the mental field and emotional life.

When using the above technique, use it creatively and conclude with a successful cycle of action. Do not become trapped in memories of the past or indulge in idle daydreaming and inner suffering. Run the process through to completion and emerge renewed.

Another approach is to write clearly your problem. This can take it from the realm of emotion to a here-now realm of realism. Write your possible solutions. Once you have decided upon a solution, do what you can to bring that solution into your experience. Many problems persist because we do not clearly define them and because we remain confused and unsettled by inner conflict. Clarify your thinking, set reasonable goals and move in the direction of their actualization.

Problems of any kind are often made easier to handle if we share them with someone who is stronger than we

Emotional Harmony

are. Perhaps you do not know of such a person who is convenient at the moment. There is always the larger life, there is always God. Turn to the larger life in times of severe challenge and say, "I just can't seem to handle this by myself. However, I have every confidence that, with You, I can face anything and emerge a better person." So very often we turn in every direction but to the very source which is the most accessible!

Problems can result in our becoming stronger or, if we do not handle ourselves in a responsible manner, the result can be weakness and pain. Let us never say, "I'm the way I am because of what happened to me." This is an irresponsible statement. Every reasonably rational person has the ability to relate to his world and learn useful lessons. Inwardly acknowledge, "The potential is within me. The potential is within me. The power of the universe if within me because I am a specialized unit of the larger life."

Renouncing the Common Barriers

There are a few characteristics shared by many human beings, regardless of their station in life or origin of birth. They are so common that we often consider them to be innate to the human condition. Few people are devoid of one or more of the following: prejudice, shame, inclination to anger, pride, tendency to judge others, and smug sense of self-righteousness. Few are devoid of certain strong dislikes, for no rational reason except that, perhaps they learned the habit from a role model. We often do things because we are behaving like others with whom we have previously related. Especially in the formative years, the models we have about us can be such a powerful influence! Yet, when we reach the age of reason, when that occurs, we should be able to discern for ourselves what is appropriate, in contrast to that which is a conditioned reaction. We do not have to reject the person after which we modeled ourselves so well; we have only to renounce the nonuseful behavior. We do not have to attempt to justify our prejudices and conditioned reactions; we have only to renounce that which is not useful to healthful function.

We might think it useful to escape from the world in order to be more self-complete. Sometimes, an occasion of retreat for the purpose of inner cleansing and renewal can be useful. But, where we are in the world scene of our choice, can be the place for us to come to terms with ourselves and all that transpires. To disconnect from the world and relationships is not useful if our purpose is to function in the world and become self-actualized. He is the master of life who awakens to a level of understanding which enables him to play his role wisely and fully.

**Anyone Can Do It:
Eight Specific Steps**

Whenever we reduce a plan of action to a formula, we usually become aware of the fact that we could have just as easily listed more or fewer steps than we did. In this present formula, we will go ahead with eight steps because it seems reasonable to do so. These suggestions are to be found in any number of programs designed to assist people to fulfill their purposes and to release the potential within them.

1. *Be on Friendly Terms With Your World* — To be on friendly terms with your world, you will have to first be on friendly terms with yourself. If you are not your own best friend, it is unlikely that you will have self-esteem and a positive outlook on life. Learn to be on friendly terms with yourself and on friendly terms with the world in which you live. Life is supportive if we give it a chance. Life will assist us if we allow it to do what it wants to do.

2. *How Are Things With You Now?* — A frequent greeting, among friends is, "What's happening?" Look

about you and ask of yourself, "What's happening?" Be honest with the answers. If you feel great, acknowledge this. If you don't feel so great, acknowledge this. Take inventory of your thoughts, attitudes, feelings, condition of health, relationships and goals.

3. *Is What You are Doing Useful?* — Is your life working the way you want it to work? Even if you are not becoming self-actualized, perhaps you have a drive in another direction. If you do, perhaps your non-useful (to higher purposes) inner activities and behavior is at least useful to your misdirected ends. If you want to be successful in all areas of your life, is what you are doing now useful to this end?

4. *What Are You Going to do About It?* — Now we get into action. We make decisions, we plan, we set goals, we agree upon a useful course of action. We no longer rest in a condition of mental-emotional stagnation. We begin to stir up the powers within us and agree to move in a positive direction with our life.

5. *Have You Really Decided?* — This is it! This is the moment of agreement. Now we decide to burn our bridges, clean up the past and present, be responsible all the way and do whatever is required of us to experience self-actualization in this life-cycle.

6. *Make No Excuses for Failure* — Once we are possessed of correct information about the nature of life, who we are, and what can be experienced by us, we absolutely refuse to make excuses for weakness or failure.

7. *Respond Only to Reward* — If you attempt in a certain direction and fail, realize that you are not a failure unless you quit. Do not grovel in self-condemnation and fault-finding. Do not wallow in self-pity and guilt. Move ahead in life and experience small gains which will reward the mind's inclination in the direction of satisfaction. With each success you become stronger and more confident. With each success you become more knowledgable and competent.

8. *Do Not Turn Back* — Winners keep going forward.

Every gain is a step in the right direction. Look back, now and then, only to correct errors and to see where you have been in relationship to where you are and where you are going.

This procedure can be used for the overcoming of habits, changing behavior, and for setting and achieving any useful goal. Share this program with a friend who is in need of an assist. Do not fall into the trap of taking on his problems, but rather, show him the way out as a result of your having been successful in the use of the principles. Let your life be the example. Be so established in wellness and your right place in life, that you can say to all who seek a better way, "Welcome to my world!"

POINTS TO REMEMBER
1. Respond to whatever is useful to your purposes, avoid all that is not useful.
2. Clear all conflict and emotional problems.
3. Be on friendly terms with a friendly universe.
4. Realize that no external condition has any power over you.
5. Renounce all barriers to self-actualization.
6. Review the eight specific steps for experiencing self-actualization.

Goal Achievement Plans
EMOTIONAL WELLNESS

Goal or Final Purpose:

Affirm: *"I will complete my puposes and achieve my goals through intelligent involvement and God's help."*

Plans for Completion and/or Achievement:

Obstacles or Restrictions, if Any:

Solutions and Plans of Action:

Affirm: *"I will use these plans and experience solutions."*

Expected Benefits as a Result of Actualizing Plans:

Purposes Completed/Goals Achieved

Completed/Achieved_____ Date_____
Completed/Achieved_____ Date_____
Completed/Achieved_____ Date_____
Record short-term gains and achievements as well as long-term gains and achievements. Use extra blank pages in this book or another sheet of paper for more complete planning.

Actualization Guidelines

Be resolved to move in the direction of maturity. Be resolved to clear all emotional conflicts and to live on friendly terms with your world. Forgive others and release them to their highest good. Forgive yourself, if need be, and release yourself to your highest good. Resolve to be goal-directed instead of problem-centered. At all times, live in the awareness that the larger life is your permanent reality. Therefore, you can always be serene and at peace within yourself in the midst of change and challenge. Do what you can to clear your emotional life and give everything to God. God knows how to solve your problems and adjust all affairs in the most rewarding manner.

Something to contemplate and realize:

"My life is lived in harmony with the flow of nature. I release all conflict and I wish myself and, others, well in all ways. I see only the good and the beautiful. Whenever I am tempted to become emotionally upset I will see through the seeming challenge and take refuge in the truth of my relationship with God."

Notes for Plans & Projects

"If anything is sacred, the human body is sacred."
— Walt Whitman

"The person whose gastric fire is well tended, who feeds it with wholesome diet, who is given to daily meditation, charity and the pursuit of spiritual salvation and who takes food and drinks that are agreeable to him, will not fall victim to approaching diseases except for special reasons. The disciplined person of one-hundred years, blessed by good men and devoid of disease."
— Ayurveda

7
Regeneration and Radiant Living

There are several practical reasons for seeing to health and vitality of the physical body. When we are healthy and vital, we feel better and our mental attitude is more optimistic. When we are healthy and vital, we can function without physical problems restricting us as we fulfill our purposes. When we are healthy and vital, the body is inclined to become more refined, allowing a greater infusion of superconscious energies to circulate. When we are healthy and vital, the creative energies we have in excess can be used by the body to build a more refined nervous system and brain structure.

Do not settle for merely feeling good; do what you can to insure regeneration, total health, function, vitality, and radiant living! There are many who work at the physical level alone, paying attention to diet and exercise, but they neglect the importance of spiritual, mental, and emotional health. True, attention to exercise, diet and rest will often pay marvelous dividends in function and a better mental and emotional condition. How superior it is, however, to attend to matters relating to health on all levels!

A person who is spiritually, mentally, and emotionally well will be inclined to live naturally in harmony with the physical universe. But, sometimes, we are tempted to emphasize positive thinking and emotional wellness, while disregarding almost entirely the basic matters relating to physical health. Health consciousness permeates the entire being and personality. Health consciousness extends into everything we do.

**Establishing
Health Consciousness**

Do not believe in the frequently shared opinion that partial function is the normal condition for human beings. Millions of people rely on drugs and medications to maintain physical comfort and, for most of these people, drugs and medications are not needed. They are, in the long term, destructive in their physical and psychological influence. In America, for instance, while almost anything and everything we might require for health and function is readily availble, a fair percentage of the population is undernourished and complains about a wide variety of physical ailments. A large percentage of the problems reported are stress related. Fatigue, general tiredness, is a common complaint. High blood pressure, asthma, arthritis, heart problems, low blood sugar, failing eyesight, migraine headaches; the list is almost without end as we attempt to catalogue the complaints reported and diagnosed.

Why, when we know how to live in harmony with natural laws, do we fail to experience health? Why, when we have available nutritious foods, do we eat incorrectly? Why, when we know the connection between mental conflict and emotional upset, in relationship to physical illness, do we maintain harmful mental and emotional conditions? It must be that many people really do not want to be healthy and functional! If they did, they would educate themselves in health matters and do all within their power to rid themselves of illness-causing conditions.

If we want to be healthy, we can be healthy. What

about physical problems which have persisted for a long time? What about problems which seem to have been somewhat inherited? Can anything be done? If we believe in the principles we now examine, if we believe in the innate power of the soul, we will not accept any condition other than total health and vitality. The intelligence which directed the formation of this body and, which has seen to its inner nourishment over the years, surely knows how to correct any condition and, repair and regenerate the systems.

Train yourself to live from the level of inner awareness and to accept, without qualifications, the ideal of perfect health. Be firmly established in health consciousness and let this awareness extend into every level of your being and body. Remember, it is life's natural inclination to flow in the direction of completion. It is not life's natural inclination to remain restricted. Remove the restrictions and the life force, directed by the innate intelligence, will see to needed inner changes so that health and function is experienced. As long as you have the will to live and to excel, do not accept limitations.

The Natural Inclination of Life to Regenerate

When we conduct our affairs as nature does, in natural cycles of rest and activity, nature has an opportunity to regenerate the body. When we become overstressed, overly tired, heavy laden with mental and emotional burdens, toxic, and improperly nourished, we are working against life's inclination in the direction of regeneration.

1. We can lower stress by meditating correctly on a regular schedule and by learning to relate to our world with understanding. We can avoid becoming overly tired by scheduling our activities and by using the creative abilities we possess with wisdom. When necessary, we can take a vacation and remove ourselves from our usual

environment so that we allow ourselves the opportunity to become refreshed and unburdened by matters which might have resulted in the accumulation of mental and emotional pressures.

2. We can see to nutrition, for our personal needs. There is no single diet that will agree with every person but, with practice, we can find the nutrition program which best serves us. The basic pattern for man, relative to nutrition, is to eat grains, seeds (beans, nuts, etc.), vegetables and fruits. Some people can handle milk and cheese and others find these dairy products not useful. Basically, one should consume foods as near to their natural condition as possible, while they are fresh and in good condition. This means that foods which are treated with chemicals, drastically altered in any way, or not in their natural condition, should be avoided. White sugar, excess salt and processed flour can be excluded. Man's body, based on a comparison of teeth and length of intestinal tract, with meat-eating and non-meat eating creatures, seems to have been designed for a vegetarian diet. The matter of food choice is personal, because the individual is the best judge of what foods and food combinations are most useful to his purposes. However, it could be useful to experiment with a non-meat diet to see if this proves to be more useful.

3. If your body is toxic because waste matter has not been properly expelled, cleanse the system. An easy way is to plan a two or three week program for this purpose and select foods which are both nutritious and regenerative. Here is an easy program. Begin the process with an enema the night before the first day's change in food intake. Throughout the program be sure the bowels are functional so that waste matter is eliminated. For breakfast eat only fresh fruit such as apples, pears or a mixture of desired fruits. Consume a reasonable portion. For lunch prepare a fresh garden salad, as much as desired, with olive oil and lemon juice as a dressing. For dinner eat another green salad and have a portion of

brown rice. Garnish the rice, if you wish, with chopped onion or soy sauce to please the palate. Continue this program for two or three weeks and notice the feeling of lightness and change in mental attitude. Notice the increase in energy. This is not an extreme routine and will result in a cleansing of waste matter from the body. After concluding the program, return to a more varied diet as personal choice dictates.

Naturally, if you are already on a diet recommended by a physician or health advisor, follow that program. In special instances, such as a low blood sugar problem, one should follow professional advice in diet matters.

Vitamin and mineral supplementation may, or may not, be useful and this should be a matter of intelligent choice. Very few of us know how to correctly diagnose our own vitamin or mineral needs. It is taught, by many in the health field, that if one is living in harmony with natural laws, the body will be provided all of its requirements through the foods eaten and will also produce within itself whatever else is required for health and function. The field of nutrition is of such large dimensions that the reader is advised, in special matters, to become involved in further research. My personal recommendation is to remain as close to a simple and natural diet as possible and avoid extremes in any instance.

Are you getting enough regular rest? Do you sleep on a reasonably regular schedule, soundly and to meet your personal requirements? The sleep cycle, like many body cycles, is usually more result-producing if we are regular in our pattern. When going to sleep, let your thoughts flow to creative possibilities or to thoughts of your relationship to God. This is not only useful for general consciousness-clearing purposes, but can result in sleep that is more superconscious than subconscious. That is, as a result of a creative and prayerful approach to sleep, superconscious influences invade the mental field, enabling us to receive guidance, solve problems, and function more effectively when we awaken. It is not unusual, for a person who falls asleep in a meditative mood, to experience vivid dreams during which expansion of awareness is the dominant perception. Eventually, as a result of clearing which takes place in the mental field, we are inclined to always be aware regardless of the prevailing mental state. During sleep we will be inwardly aware and during waking moments, when fully involved with external matters, we will be anchored in inner knowing.

When stress is released from the nervous system and physical body, the healing currents are able to flow without interference. We are then more likely to live our entire span of life on earth in a healthy and youthful condition. I know of men and women in their eighth and ninth decade of Earth experience who are as alert, mentally capable, and as physically active as many people in their middle years. All of these physically older, but young in mind and body, people enjoy living and know how to remain free from mental and psychological pressures. They are active and goal-directed. They are happy and have a sense of attunement with the larger life of which they are an expression.

**The Ideal Exercise
for Your Personal Needs**

The ideal exercise program for you is the one that brings you the results you want. Exercise tones the muscles, improves blood circulation, increases energy reserves, aids in general body function and helps us to feel more alive and in tune with the world. You may find that a daily routine of stretching and limbering movements is helpful. You may find that fast walking or slow running is suitable to you. Swimming is a good all around exercise program. Tennis, hiking the hills, riding a bicycle, and rebounding on a small trampoline are other popular ways to exercise the body and refresh the mental outlook. Recommended by many health experts is vigorous excercise, two or three times a week, to the point of causing the heart to beat faster for at least twenty minutes during the exercise period. This contriutes to health of the heart and circulatory system and improves body function as a whole.

Hatha Yoga asanas and breathing exercises to promote the circulation of vital force throughout the system is extremely popular. The practice of *yogasanas*, as the poses are called, have the effect of slowing down body processes and contributing to relaxation and reduction in stress. They also contribute to the function of the endocrine glands, aid in calming the mind and prepare us for concentration and meditation. The twisting and stretching poses improve lymphatic circulation, blood circulation and the circulation of nerve force. The breathing exercises are designed to give control over vital force, prana, and to assist this force to flow through subtle channels in the body without interference.

Chiropractic adjustments, if available, can be useful because nerve force is often restricted along the spine and into the body because of interference caused by improper vertebral alignment. There are many procedures available if one needs the assistance of a professional in the matter of health care.

At all times, take the healthy-minded approach to matters relative to improvement and better function of the body. If we do not have a basic health consciousness, we may be inclined to try one system after another in a vain attempt to find solutions to problems. I stress the total approach; spiritual health, mental clarity, emotional wellness and any useful program that one might feel led to do to contribute to physical health. Once we have seen to health and function, we have but to observe the basic procedures which are useful to our purposes and devote the major portion of our time and energies to achieving goals and experiencing fulfillment. Some people become so obsessed with matters relating to health and function that they have no time or inclination to be involved with the process of living a happy, creative life.

**If You Need Healing
and Improved Function**

If your body is not functioning as it is designed to function, healing and correction is needed. A host of ailments are directly related to mental and emotional conflict. (See the chapters in this book in which these areas are handled in more complete detail if an assist is needed in these areas.) Hypertension is the cause of many ailments. Heal the tendency to become overstressed and the symtoms are likely to fade away. Is your thinking clear and orderly? Are you really emotionally well? Have you seen to proper nutrition, rest and excercise?

Perhaps healing is needed because the mental-emotional patterns have to be changed, or because the body energies are not circulating as strongly as they should. Use the technique of creative visualization to inwardly see and feel yourself in a healthy condition. Cooperate with the innate intelligence, which is inclined to insure health and function if given the opportunity to do what it will. Picture yourself in perfect health, with all systems and organs functioning perfectly. Send vital force to the body parts in need of regeneration. Inwardly lovingly accept and bless your body. Feel happy, healthy and grateful for health and function. Smile more often, be relaxed and cheerful, laugh more.

We do not have to try too hard to cause health and function. A better approach is to expect to be healthy, feel healthy, make plans for the near and distant future and call upon the healing forces which already lie dormant within you. Can you accept health and function? Will you accept health and function? Often, when working with another who is in need of assistance in the direction of health, we ask, "Do you want to be well and healthy?" If we can elicit an affirmative response and succeed in getting the person to agree upon a constructive plan of action, we can usually predict positive response. The will-to-live is the most powerful healing influence in the world, because the will-to-live promotes energies and processes of the body in the direction of regeneration, health and vitality. When the will-to-live is absent, life forces become more diminished in their flows and move in the direction of being dormant.

Our lives are lived in stages and cycles. We came into this world and we are moving through stages of growth, experience and responsibility. When we have fulfilled our purpose here we will move from this plane of experience and continue to another. As long as we are relating to this world, our creative opportunities continue and our responsibilities to self and others remain. Isn't it a useful idea to be as healthy and vital as possible while we are here? Isn't it a useful plan to continue consciously in a relationship with the larger life which is ever-expanding? I think this way and I'm sure you do, too.

No matter your needs, whatever your requirements for health and wellness, you have the means to these ends in this world in which you presently dwell and you have the inner knowing to make wise choices every step of the way.

POINTS TO REMEMBER
1. **It is natural to be healthy, functional and vital.**
2. **See to health and function on all levels.**
3. **Be established in health consciousness.**
4. **Meditate to release stress from the nervous system and body.**
5. **Attend to nutritional needs and to body needs.**
6. **Schedule an exercise program to suit your personal requirements.**
7. **Release the vital force to allow healing and function.**

Goal Achievement Plans
HEALTH & VITALITY

Goal or Final Purpose:

Affirm: *"I will complete my puposes and achieve my goals through intelligent involvement and God's help."*

Plans for Completion and/or Achievement:

Obstacles or Restrictions, if Any:

Solutions and Plans of Action:

Affirm: *"I will use these plans and experience solutions."*

Expected Benefits as a Result of Actualizing Plans:

Purposes Completed/Goals Achieved

Completed/Achieved _____ Date _____
Completed/Achieved _____ Date _____
Completed/Achieved _____ Date _____

Record short-term gains and achievements as well as long-term gains and achievements. Use extra blank pages in this book or another sheet of paper for more complete planning.

Actualization Guidelines

Be good to yourself. If you respect yourself you will naturally do all that is useful to allow life to nourish and bless you. Your body is an extension of you. Find that program which best suits your personal needs in relationship to diet, exercise, rest and rejuvenation. Live out of soul awareness, always, and harmonize with natural laws as you understand them. Accept health, vitality and long life as natural. Be aware of your purpose in this world and realize that an enlightened consciousness extends fully into your physical form. At the soul level you are already vital. Allow this vitality to permeate every system, every organ, every tissue and every cell of your body.

Something to contemplate and realize:

"I joyously accept health and vitality as my natural experience. I easily discard all attitudes and activities which are not in accord with radiant livng. Infinite life floods my mind, feeling nature and physical form to insure perfect function and glowing health."

"I have never found the companion that was so companionable as solitude. We are for the most part more lonely when we go abroad among men than when we stay in our chambers. A man thinking or working is always alone, let him be where he will."
- Henry David Thoreau

"Thou shalt love the Lord thy God with all thy heart, and with all thy soul, and with all thy mind. This is the first and great commandment. And the second is like unto it, Thou shalt love thy neighbor as thyself."
- Matthew 22:37-39

"They helped every one his neighbor; and every one said to his brother, Be of good courage."
- Isiah 41:6

8
Experiencing Open and Supportive Relationships

There is not a person anywhere in the universe who does not need a relationship, either with others of his kind, or with the environment in which he lives. In a society there is need for mutually supportive interaction between individuals and groups making up that society and, when a person is alone with nature, there is need for cooperation with those aspects of nature which enable one to survive and function. Human beings need to relate in a supportive way to other people and to their environment.

In the ideal relationship, there is a sharing for mutual good and to meet needs. At a selfish level we may see interelationships as a trade-off, a matter of taking by common consent. On a higher level, we understand that life is one organic whole and that a nourishing flow between all elements of this whole is required if the world organism is to be healthy. In a healthy family unit, love and support is shared between all members of the unit. Likewise, in a society, an organization, the global community as a whole.

The basis of open and supportive relationships is understanding and love. When we understand that life is an organic whole, we can no longer be self-centered. We think, instead, of doing all we can to improve the condition of life as we know it. When we love, when we feel a kinship with all life and a respect for all life, we are inclined naturally to share ourselves in the most useful manner. Behind every appearance, in all situations and in all life expressions, there is the one life endeavoring to unfold and fulfill purposes. As we see this, we are more responsive to the needs of others and to the needs of our planet. We sometimes think it easier to love nature and the plant and animal kingdom than to love our fellow human beings. Many human beings, complex and unpredictable, seem directed by ego-needs and fear. We can, with practice, look past all surface personality traits and acknowledge the essence of other people. We can refrain from prejudicial judgements, and respect that essence which is as divine as ourselves.

Developing Communication Skills and Abilities

Communication begins with the individual. If we are clear mentally and emotionally, we will clearly perceive our environment. We will see what is before us instead of screening our perceptions through mental and emotional distortions. A person who is directed toward failure will see about him only reasons to fail. A person who is resentful will see only situations to enable him to be more resentful. One who is directed toward fulfillment will see opportunity at every turn, and will look for the good and the beautiful in all circumstances. Of prime importance, is our own spiritual and psychological health if we are to communicate effectively with others.

Communicate with your immediate environment. Accept the world about you as a supportive energy-realm which is designed to provide you with all you require for security and happiness while you are here. Respect your environment and be a good steward of the things and resources for which you are responsible. How long has it been since you have taken a walk and consciously been aware of your surroundings? How long has

Supportive Relationships

it been since you have allowed yourself the opportunity to be close to nature and to absorb the healing influences of the fresh air, the sun and growing things? How long has it been since you have actually communicated with your automobile, your clothes, your house or apartment, your working tools? Things are energy-formed and respond to our attention and care. We might even say, they respond to our pure love.

A major problem between people is lack of communication. Do we speak clearly when we communicate with another? Do we write clearly? Do we really send the correct signals? Do we listen to people? Do we really hear what they are attempting to share with us? When we desire clear communication there must be: something to communicate, an agreement about what is being communicated, and an acknowledgement that the communication has been clearly received. Without all three — intention, agreement and acknowledgement — the communication cycle is not complete and error is present. Remove error and communication is experienced.

When we are discerning, we can be aware of the intention of others through intuition. Even if a verbal or written attempt is not clear, we can learn to discern the intention of another and understand his purpose. We have all experienced occasions when words were unnecessary, when the silent flow was sufficient. If you say, "I just can't seem to communicate my intentions clearly," realize that communication skills can be learned and abilities can be acquired. Practice creative visualization and inwardly see yourself in situations which were a challenge and run through a scene that would imply success and completion in communication with another. In this way you will gain confidence and train yourself before you confront what was formerly a challenging situation.

When attempting to communicate with a person who is hostile, or who is suspicious of your motives, put him at ease by assuring him through words and manner, that you are supportive and cooperative. Everyone wants to be respected, supported and assisted in some way. To enter into an open and supportive relationship with others, see to it that you are respectful, supportive and helpful in all ways. The marvelous thing is that when we give to life the best we are, the best is given to us.

Clearing Relationships:
Past and Present

Current communication problems may have their roots in past incidents and experiences. If we have been rejected, hurt or abused in a past relationship, we may avoid open communication in order to avoid more rejection, hurt or abuse. Pray your way through any problem related to past incidents which have caused you hurt. If the persons involved in the incident are still alive, it may be useful to communicate with them and clear the problem. Perhaps we have not overcome our fear of parental authority. Perhaps we are still trying to prove something to them. Perhaps we are making a mess of our lives just to spite them. Strange reasons, of course, but our reactions are often other than what is the ideal. Come to terms with memories and feelings of past failure, rejection, loss and pain and, in this way, liberate the energy for a higher purpose.

Clear all inner restrictions to the best of your ability. Some basic restrictions have their origin in our early years. Perhaps we fear life? Perhaps we fear death? Perhaps we fear success? Perhaps we fear the opinions of others? Examine your fears and clear your mind and emotional nature relative to them. Many people have conflict because, while they desire fulfillment, they feel guilty about being happy and prosperous. More than one person has informed me, "I am happy, I am loved, I am successful. I know it can't last forever." I know of a woman who was married to a man who was rich. She had everything she had ever wanted in a relationship.

Supportive Relationships

She would say, privately, "It just seems too good to be true. I feel I am living in a dream." Later, her husband lost his money and they divorced. When I last heard from her she was doing domestic work to provide for herself. We always externalize our own states of consciousness, because we are working in harmony with a responsive mind which is attuned to our mental and emotional conditions.

If a relationship in the present is in need of healing, see to that healing. Frequently, when others in the relationship seem to be so stubborn, it is because we have persisted in maintaining a mental picture of them as we see them. We may not be willing to change until they change, therefore, we have an impasse. We have heard people say, "I'll change if you will change, but, you have to change first." So many times our communication problems persist because we insist upon dramatizing our own personality games.

We often play games, don't we? We dramatize to others through our mannerisms, our speech, our response. We play the games we do because we find them useful to our purposes. Our purposes may be to keep the game of conflict going, for one psychological reason or another. And, so it seems, there are some people who were born mean and nasty. No person has to persist in any pattern just because the pattern has been running for a duration of time. Change can always be introduced, if there is a willingness on the part of the person to change. Even if another with whom we relate is mean and spiteful, it is up to us to maintain our inner calm and do the appropriate thing in all circumstances. We may not approve of a person's attitude or behavior, but we can always respect the inner spirit.

A most useful practice for the purpose of maintaining clear relationships is that of keeping an agreement once one has been made. If we agree to do something, we should do it, on time and in the manner agreed upon. When we keep agreements, we maintain clear communication and prove to others that we are dependable and supportive. To let another person down, once we have entered into an agreement, is to be irresponsible to the final degree. Keeping of agreements extends to little things: arriving for appointments on time, returning telephone calls, handling our personal responsibilities in a group situation. In short, being there when we are supposed to be there.

**In All Relationships
Everyone Can Benefit**

In all relationships, personal, social, business or whatever, all who are involved can experience mutual benefit if the relationship is ideal. You do not have to lose for someone to gain. You do not have to gain at another person's expense. We emphasize *supportive* because it is our duty to support and nourish our environment. In the game of life everyone can win. What about the losers, who seem to be many? They can be taught to win. We can inspire, instruct, motivate and call forth the best of which others are capable if we will but do so. We cannot always predict the form in which their growth will take, because they have their inner needs and patterns with which to contend. There is no reason why we cannot envision an ideal human society and an ideal world condition and work for it by seeing to our own fulfillment and then sharing ourselves with others.

Parents can live an ideal life so that their children will have useful models after which to style their own lives. Parents can teach children the wisdom of respect, duty, attention to detail, education and intelligent planning for the future. It is our duty to assist those who follow us and to share with them our understanding.

Men and women can learn to respect and nourish each other and to assist personal growth and unfoldment. When we really respect and love another person we naturally wish the highest and best for them, not al-

Supportive Relationships

ways what we think is highest and best for them. Have you ever said to someone, "I want the best for you, but I do wish you would do what I think is best for you"? A person might say, "I'd be happier if you were a doctor instead of a salesman." Compassion and a desire to assist others sometimes causes us to try to make decision for them, decisions which they should have the freedom to make for themselves.

Spiritual and emotional maturity naturally result in open and supportive relationships. We would not think of injuring another if we saw that person as another expression of ourselves. We would not think of polluting our environment, if we realized fully that our environment is supportive of us and will be the home for future world citizens.

Sexuality: Our Own and the World's

The world exists because of interchange between male and female influences. Even at the level of the atom we find relationships between positive and negative influences. In nature we witness urge and fulfillment, desire and satisfaction, tension and relaxation. Life is like this and we are involved with the life process. Males in the animal and human kingdoms have what females need and females have what males need. When we examine the ways in which nature has unfolded, the whole process is really quite extraordinary. Male and female interchange is necessary if health and harmony is to be experienced. Some people have arrived at a condition of such inner balance that their own internal maleness and femaleness has resulted in a degree of self-completion. They still, however, have to relate to the maleness and femaleness of the world about them.

It should be the most natural thing in the world for a person to come to terms with his own sexuality but, if we believe the reports, many men and women suffer from conflicts and difficulties in this aspect of their lives. People in love have few conflicts, because nature is so designed that, when allowed, she takes her course in the direction of completion. Faulty education sometimes results in feelings of guilt relative to sexuality but correct education, self-analysis and common sense will usually put matters right.

The sexual urge is powerful and seeks expression through intimacy, mutual sharing and a relationship leading in the direction of fulfillment. Although modern society has been deluged with books about how to work at experiencing a satisfying relationship, healthy-minded adults need little else than their own gift of inner understanding to handle themselves in relationship to their own sexuality and the world's. If we care about ourselves and if we care about those with whom we relate, honesty and mutual support is certain to be the rule. Through the law of sexual attraction, nature has provided for the perpetuation of the species and the emotional and psychological fulfillment of living beings. It is not for nothing that philosophers and poets of the ages have extolled the virtues of love and deep communion between male and female. The larger life expresses through us to glorify its highest ends.

A truly loving relationship in no way interferes with growth and self-actualization. On the contrary, the ability to love, and support others is evidence of health and wellness. There can be no mean feeling or behavior when love prevails. There can be no jealousy, resentment or any destructive or nonuseful thought or desire when love is present. Perfect love, in all relationships, is the answer to every challenge, the solution to every ill.

The Golden Years as Maturing & Sharing Years

When life has been well lived, we can move into the final years of our life on earth in the full bloom of maturity. This can be an occasion for completing cycles of action, for final clearing of mind and consciousness, and for preparing to depart this realm for another. A self-actualized person does not shrink from the closing of one phase of experience, because he knows that a new phase is certain. If one has learned well his lessons as a result of handling responsibilities and fulfilling destiny, he is then in a stable position to share his knowledge with others. The ideal is to become established in a successful living pattern in the early adult years, and then engage in philanthropic works to assist society in the direction of greater health and to enlighten civilization. Even among members of family and friends an older, wiser, person is supportive and naturally sharing when maturity is experienced. Of course, many older people still retain rigid attitudes, but there are many in their golden years whose knowledge is overlooked by younger members of the community.

The laws of mind and consciousness do not cease to work for us just because we reach a certain physical age. Let no person fall into the trap of thinking in terms of limitation and restriction of any kind as the later years are approached. A useful thing for anyone to do, is to encourage persons who are older to think in the direction of remaining creative and functional. Many older people report that, from there point of view, life gets better and better as the years roll by. Such men and women report that they love more freely, feel just as strongly, are as curious about life as ever before and that their vital forces continue unabated. In some areas of western society, and in some cultures of the world, old age is respected, even revered. This is a beautiful and wholesome attitude to be cultivated by members of the human community.

And, as it must to all world-involved souls, the time will come when one must say farewell to this sphere because the journey has ended and new experiences await. We were born into this world as a result of having left another, and when we depart this world we will enter yet another. Life is like this, life continues its evolutionary way and no amount of wishful thinking can stay the process. If we have lived well, we will make our departure well and we will flow easily into the light of consciousness from which we once emerged, consciously and in total peace and serenity. We will have left the world a better place for our having been here. There will be no regrets, no loose ends unattended, nothing left undone that should have been done. We leave behind our good works and, perhaps, projects others have inherited, but we continue our unfolding experience without a backward glance.

A word to you who have a relationship with a person whose life on earth is ending. Do not attempt to hold them back and do not confuse them with selfish demands. Love them, bless them and allow the freedom and solitude, if they desire it, to make needed inner preparations for their next step to fulfillment.

Our early years on earth are for becoming acquainted with our new environment and for preliminary education. During our young adult years we have the opportunity to further learn, to experiment, to prepare for the adult phase. In the adult world we enter into agreements and contracts, fulfill our obligations to society and find our chosen place in the overall plan. Later, we share our knowledge and our resources with a generous world. Finally, we settle our affairs in order to enter the final phase.

We are Relating to Consciousness, Always

In all of our relationships, we are relating to consciousness in various forms and aspects of expression. It may seem that we are relating to people, to nature, to things and events, but we are not. People, nature, things and events are surface occurances on the screen of time and space. All surface appearances will change, but consciousness will never change. When we are anchored in this understanding, we are able to play whatever role inclined, well and with enjoyment, because we see the overall picture. Our outlook becomes cosmic, our appreciation for the total process greater, and the larger life is then able to unfold its grand potential with little or no resistance. The most practical person, the most realistic man or woman, must eventually awaken to a sense of wonder upon observing the procession of events that pass before us. Finally, conscious realization is experienced and one understands that he is both the observer and the participant, the audience and the actor, and he has, in a small way, assisted in the planning and the production of the play.

When we experience even a small measure of success in our attempts to more openly and supportively communicate with our world, we will be rewarded for the attempts we have made and inspired to continue until fulfillment is ours.

POINTS TO REMEMBER
1. **All relationships should be mutually supportive.**
2. **Develop communication skills and abilities.**
3. **Clear all problems with others and your environment.**
4. **Do not play psychological games. Be open, honest and helpful.**
5. **Come to terms with your own sexuality.**
6. **Remember, we are always relating to consciousness.**

Goal Achievement Plans
SUPPORTIVE RELATIONSHIPS

Goal or Final Purpose:

Affirm: *"I will complete my puposes and achieve my goals through intelligent involvement and God's help."*

Plans for Completion and/or Achievement:

Obstacles or Restrictions, if Any:

Solutions and Plans of Action:

Affirm: *"I will use these plans and experience solutions."*

Expected Benefits as a Result of Actualizing Plans:

Purposes Completed/Goals Achieved

Completed/Achieved _____ Date _____
Completed/Achieved _____ Date _____
Completed/Achieved _____ Date _____

Record short-term gains and achievements as well as long-term gains and achievements. Use extra blank pages in this book or another sheet of paper for more complete planning.

Actualization Guidelines

Be attuned to your world. See needs and fill them. Think in terms of service, of cooperation, of loving and supportive relationships. Think in terms of assisting others to fulfill their purposes as they move in the direction of their destined good. Be on open terms with the energies in nature, all living things and with every person with whom you have a relationship. Rejoice in the good fortune of others. Let life meet the needs of others through you. Let yourself be nourished and blessed through others. See through all personality appearances and recognize the divine nature of each person. We are all one family in consciousness. We share a common source, we share common goals, we share common ends. Planetary consciousness is cleared and becomes more healthy as we truly love and allow ourselves to be loved.

Something to contemplate and realize:

"I respect myself and I respect other people. I acknowledge that life is benevolent and supportive and I am open to life's goodness and to life's supportive influence. With each passing day I become more conscious, more loving and more open to life. I appreciate this opportunity to rejoice in the awareness of the goodness of life."

"Beloved, I wish above all things that thou mayest prosper and be in health, even as thy soul prospereth."
- *3 John 2*

"Physical concepts are free creations of the human mind, and are not, however it may seem uniquely determined by the external world."
- *Albert Einstein*

"In the world of physics we watch a shadowgraph performance of the drama of familiar life. The shadow of my elbow rests on the shadow table as the shadow ink flows over the shadow paper. It is all symbolic, and as a symbol the physicist leaves it. Then comes the alchemist Mind who transmutes the symbols. . To put the conclusion crudely, the stuff of the world is mind-stuff."
- *Sir Arthur Stanley Eddington*
The Nature of the Physical World

9

True and Lasting Prosperity for You

Are you thriving? Are you flourishing? Are you successful in each and every area of your life? If so, you are prospering as you were intended to prosper. If there is any area of your life in which you are not thriving, flourishing and being successful, decide now to put an end to all restrictions and limitations.

Once, during a seminar, I opened the discussion to the theme of prosperity. Various reactions were immediately evident. Many in the group were interested in the theme, a few were disinterested, some were a little upset because I had introduced the theme into a program announced as one during which self-realization and self-actualization would be stressed. Among those who were interested in the theme, were men and women who shared openly their challenges and their dreams. Among the few who were disinterested, were persons who were either satisfied with their lot in life, or who did not think the theme relative to the purpose of self-actualization. Among those who were upset, were persons who felt guilty about having a comfortable lifestyle, or who felt that the theme was not appropriate to discuss during a seminar which emphasized spiritual matters.

If we are to experience the unfoldment and actualization of our innate abilities, we must come to terms with the world in which we function. All areas and aspects of life must be examined and handled. There are many people who are intelligent, healthy, and who experience wholesome and supportive relationships with others who are not able to achieve their goals or do what they really feel led to do, because they are not able to come to terms with things, planned events and resources. Many can plan a project, bring almost all necessary parts of the plan together, and then fail because they are not able to be open to the flow of life. They can begin ventures and proceed up to a point, but beyond that they cannot move. They may be afraid of success. They may have failed to use all of the steps in their plan of action. They may be afraid to handle responsibility. They may be unable to be open to the flow of money. The basic problem is, they have not yet come into the ideal mental attitude and state of consciousness to enable them to function freely in relationship to all aspects of their world.

Life wants to express through us, but unless we cooperate with life's inclination, we will not move in harmony with the available trends and circumstances. Examine your inner attitudes to see if you are harboring any resistances to be prosperous. Do you think it not right to be successful? Do you think in terms of limitation? Are you afraid of any possible changes a prosperous lifestyle might cause? Are you basically a lazy person? Do you make excuses for failure? Realize that the world in which we live is energy, and there is no increase or decrease in energy. Energy changes form, but energy is always present to take form. We can call upon an inexhaustible reserve of available energy, which will take whatever form required, if we will but first make the inner adjustment in attitude and state of consciousness. What it comes down to is this; if we want to be truly prosperous we must have a prosperity consciousness. We have to be open to the flow and we must be responsible for handling the substance of this world in an intelligent

Prosperity

manner. If we have never prospered, we can learn to prosper because there are definite laws regarding living a prosperous life. As with all other goals, all other purposes, we have to want to experience prosperity, and we have to be willing to do whatever is necessary to fall in line with the laws which govern prosperity.

Be Open to Your Good Right Where You Are

Prosperity opportunities are all around us, and we overlook them. The very things we need to use in order to experience prosperity are already available to us. The potential within us can unfold as talents, abilities and insights which can enable us to work with available outer materials in whatever useful manner we are inspired to handle. Do we think in terms of service to other people? A time-worn adage is, "Find a need and fill it," but this alone will not satisfy us if we are thinking in terms of true, long-term service. Human beings have many wants and needs, and almost anyone can prosper to a degree by filling those wants and needs. One on the self-actualization path thinks in terms of what is useful to the health and wellness of others, as well as in terms of filling needs. Perhaps you can fill a real human need in a way that has never been done before. Perhaps the quality and character of the service you can render to others is unique. Perhaps you can render a service that is already being rendered, but do it in a better, more useful way. Find real human needs and fill them. Remember, service to others means that we are blessed as we serve, and the person served is enriched.

If you are in business, or rendering service for which there is a fee expected, be open to just and fair compensation. You are worthy of fair return for the service you render to others. Be open to the flow that returns to you as compensation for your service. Be also open to unplanned flow, because blessings can manifest in many ways other than through the channels we have established. Life seems to pour out a lavish flow of goodness upon those who are fully involved with the idea of service.

Creative enterprise is not incompatible with enlightened living. In fact, enlightened men and women function at all levels of society. Some are led to be involved in work and duty which is not related to a large number of people. Others are led to direct vast business organizations, go into politics, enter the ministry and, in whatever way, follow their own star. High or low, famous or unknown, has nothing to do with personal prosperity and personal fulfillment as long as one is in his right place and is doing what he feels is his destined duty. That person is a success who is doing what he does, because he wants to do it, and feels that he is rendering the best possible service by doing what he does. That person is prosperous who is happily engaged in a worthwhile activity for which he feels best suited.

If a person wants to be famous, he can be famous. If he wants to be rich in the world's goods, he can be rich; but, if he is not in his right place in the overall scheme, if he is not doing what he is best suited to do, he is not truly prosperous regardless of the outer trappings and signs of success. I would inspire you to find your right place in life and to move into the stream of grace which, alone, can result in everlasting freedom and true prosperity.

Discipline is required in every area of living, including that of properly relating to our chosen vocation and mode of service. Valuable training, always, is to be disciplined in all areas, and this will result in disciplined behavior in matters of business and creative enterprise. Do we make wise use of things, of money, of time and energy? A person may be careful with things and reasonably wise in the use of time and energy, but waste money. Money is a convenient form of energy which we convert to goods and services. What we have to do when we spend money, is to think in terms of whether or not we are prudent in the manner in which we convert it to goods and services. Are we investing our time, energy and money, or are we squandering our resources? Learn to be realistic about such matters without allowing yourself to fall into the pattern of thinking in terms of limitation or lack.

**Prosperity Can Be
a Family Affair**

When a group of people in a domestic relationship or a business one share a group consciousness, it is important that everyone work together for a common cause. Areas of interest may vary, but a group of people are interdependent and they mix attitudes, moods and states of consciousness. Sometimes, just one person in a group of otherwise creative and prosperity conscious men and women, can undermine the effectiveness of the group purpose. Negative attitudes are contagious just as are positive ones. Therefore, do what you can to insure the psychological health of everyone in your group.

In a family situation, it may be that only one person is actively involved in a vocation through which income is realized. Others in the family unit should not think in terms of limiting their good to the efforts of one person. If nonworking members of the family unit unfold their own respective prosperity consciousness, either the working member will realize a larger flow of compensation for service rendered, or new avenues through which good can flow will open. One of the most limiting of all attitudes is that of thinking in terms of a fixed income. This occurs frequently among people who work for an hourly wage, are on a salary, or have retired and are receiving income from investments or social security benefits. Nothing is fixed in this universe! The only place anything is fixed and limited is in a person's belief and attitude!

Ordering Your Financial Affairs

While leaving yourself open to unplanned good fortune, while planning newer and better ways to render service, make wise use of available resources and move into the flow of life. Think, if you like, in terms of rendering service and being compensated, think in terms of being open to all of the good the universe wants to provide, but do not think in terms of giving to receive. Some people begin at this level of thinking and, to a degree, the process seems to work. The problem with this approach is that one is often tempted to fall into the pattern of bargaining with life. Of course, life is more than willing to bargain with us on our terms, but there is a higher way. This higher way is to give to life the best of which you are capable, and be open to life as life unfolds in limitless proportion. Life flows through us and to the degree that we are open to this flow, to this degree it will express. The moment of giving, the moment of sharing, the moment of rendered service, is the very moment of blessing. We are prospered the very moment we are able to give of ourselves to life, in whatever manner and in whatever capacity.

Learn to be appreciative to life. Be thankful for the opportunity to experience and express yourself. Be thankful for the blessings you now enjoy. What is praised tends to magnify, and what is faulted tends to diminish. Through the power of the thoughts you think, and the words you speak, you can call forth abundance in your personal life and in the lives of others. Practice this in little ways, to test the principle. You will see that when you give your constructive attention to something its condition improves and, when you envision the worst, conditions become worsened. Express your appreciation to life by sharing positive ideas, constructive comments, a smile, faith in others, and your resources for worthy causes. As you do this, life moves through you in greater measure and you naturally experience uplift and true prosperity.

If at all possible, retain a portion of your income for the purpose of personal investment. If you need to do so, retain the services of a qualified expert in the field of investments. Be practical in the use of the money you earn or receive through various channels. Money can be wasted, it can be unwisely used, or it can be profitably invested. Money is energy, and with this money-energy you can extend your influence and do many worthwhile things. I knew of a person who once loaned money to a friend who said his business plan was fool-proof. The person never received a return from the money invested. He said, to a counselor, "I felt so good about the plan that I felt it was God's way of opening the door to greater prosperity for me!" Unless we are skilled in the matter of investments, we are wise to seek advice from a professional who knows more than we.

Use a portion of your income, or your resources, for the good of society and for some enlightenment cause. We may not be directly involved in working with people in need or with people who are seeking a better way of life, but we can channel some of our financial energy into organizations and groups through which people are well served. When you do this, feel that you are but doing your duty to assist mankind on its upward way. Feel that you are fulfilling a portion of your personal responsibility. Do not wait until some possible future time when your financial conditon is better than it is now. Begin now to invest a portion of your income for personal use in the future, and begin now to share a portion with others. Haven't we often been helped by other people, in so many ways, without having had an opportunity to say, "Thank you," or to express our appreciation? Share a portion of yourself in a positive manner. You will not only feel good about it, but you will be fulfilling your obligation to the human race.

Spend freely, but avoid waste whenever possible. The

energy of the universe circulates all around you and through you. Even though we know that energy is never exhausted, we are still responsible for the wise use of energy available to us. It is common knowledge, among those who research the habits of the majority in industrialized populations, that among working people, a large percentage of them will not save enough money or invest enough money from their earnings during their working career, to be able to provide for themselves when they retire. A major reason for this is lack of planning and the unwise use of resources over the years. Some researchers are of the opinion that ninety percent of the working class fall into this catagory.

The percentage of available funds we choose to invest, and to give to worthy causes, is a matter of personal decision. A popular practice is to use ten percent for investments and ten percent for sharing with others. Some begin with a smaller amount and others with a larger sum. However much we decide to direct into these areas, let it be regular and let it be done with an open and constructive mental attitude. I have heard of some people who are able to channel ninety percent of their income into humanity betterment causes, either through personal giving or through foundations. One thing is certain, we will never be truly prosperous until we learn to participate freely with life.

**Rejoice in the Good
Fortune of Others**

How we respond to the success or failure of other people reflects the condition of our spiritual, mental and emotional health. When we see another person experiencing good fortune, are we happy or are we envious? Do we think for a moment that the good fortune of another in any way diminishes our own? The greater the number of prosperous people in our world, the healthier our world is and will be. I am referring to health in all areas of human life. Where there is poverty in any form, there is need of healing. Where there is poverty in any form, there is error in understanding and error in relationship to life. See to it that you experience true and lasting prosperity as a conscious being and in all areas of your life. Be spiritually aware, mentally functional, emotionally well, physically vital, supportive and loving in your relationships, and able to move freely in this realm of time and space.

We do not always need to think in terms of having money to move through space and do the things we want to do. Our mental pictures are externalized in our world, therefore, learn to visualize yourself in the circumstances you desire to experience. If you want to travel to a distant place, see yourself as being there and the way will be opened to you. If you want to attract compatible friends and co-workers, see yourself in their company and they will find you. Every realistic desire contains the pattern and the energy to unfold and complete itself. If we have a useful dream, a worthwhile goal, the people and the resources necessary for its actualization will be brought together in a harmonious manner. We limit ourselves by indulging in petty thoughts; we liberate ourselves by opening ourselves to the benevolence of the universe. What is it you want to do? What is it you feel led to do for yourself and for others? You have only to clearly define it, believe in the realness of it, and open yourself to the potential of life itself.

What Would You do if all Things Were Possible?

What would you do if you had all of the money, all of the resources, all of the talent and ability in this very moment to express yourself and to engage in a useful project? Make a list of the things you would really like to do, how you will begin and when you will experience completion. Let your imagination take you as far as you want to go in this planning process. Some of the most impossible dreams have come true. Play this game of make-believe with yourself, and open the windows of your mind, the potential of your soul, to see what an awakening effect it will have upon you. Perhaps your dreams are important only to you. Perhaps they are important to others. One thing is certain; the greater our understanding of our relationship with life, and the more we are responsive to life's inclination in the direction of unfoldment, the more we are attuned to the course of destined good.

Perhaps all of your goals will not be achieved. Perhaps you will later modify your plans. Perhaps you will meet with barriers and restrictions because you are ahead of your time. It does not matter; the more you awaken and use the power within you, the happier you will be and the more you will have grown in the direction of your potential.

POINTS TO REMEMBER
1. Are you thriving, flourishing and being successful?
2. Cooperate with life's inclination in the direction of fulfillment.
3. Be open to your good right where you are.
4. Discipline yourself in every area and aspect of your life.
5. See to the prosperity of your family and friends.
6. Put order into your financial affairs.
7. Rejoice in the happiness and success of others.

Goal Achievement Plans
PROSPERITY

Goal or Final Purpose:

Affirm: *"I will complete my puposes and achieve my goals through intelligent involvement and God's help."*

Plans for Completion and/or Achievement:

Obstacles or Restrictions, if Any:

Solutions and Plans of Action:

Affirm: *"I will use these plans and experience solutions."*

Expected Benefits as a Result of Actualizing Plans:

Purposes Completed/Goals Achieved

Completed/Achieved_____ Date_____
Completed/Achieved_____ Date_____
Completed/Achieved_____ Date_____

Record short-term gains and achievements as well as long-term gains and achievements. Use extra blank pages in this book or another sheet of paper for more complete planning.

Actualization Guidelines

Accept without reservation that it is life's natural inclination to thrive, to flourish, to be successful. Accept without reservation that you are destined to thrive, to flourish and to be successful. To prosper in all ways is natural. To fail to prosper is not natural. Be attuned to the natural urge of life and prosper in all ways. Be established in a prosperity consciousness. Prove yourself by doing all that you are led to do to experience prosperity. Trust life. Trust the principles of mind and consciousness. Trust nature. Renounce fear completely and live by faith. Make wise use of your available resources and be open to the flow which has its origin in the inexaustible ocean of unmanifest consciousness. Do not wait until a future time to put prosperity principles into practice. The potential is within you. Let this inborn potential become fully expressive in all areas of your life experience.

Something to contemplate and realize:

"Without grasping at things, and without fearing to handle the substance of this world, I live confidently in harmony with the laws of prosperity. I make wise use of the resources at hand while I remain open to the goodness of life. I fully realize that life meets me at my level of personal need, on time and always in abundance. As I experience increasing prosperity in my life I bless others in their prosperity experiences."

Notes for Plans & Projects

"Ye are the light of the world. A city that is set on an hill cannot be hid. Neither do men light a candle, and put it under a bushel, but on a candlestick, and it giveth light unto all that are in the house. Let your light so shine before men, that they may see your good works, and glorify your Father which is in heaven."
- *Matthew 5:14-16*

"The more wise and powerful the master; the more directly is his work created, and the simpler it is."
- *Meister Eckhart*

"When I consider thy heavens, the work of thy fingers, the moon and the stars, which thou hast ordained; What is man, that thou art mindful of him? and the son of man, that thou visitest him? For thou hast made him a little lower than the angels, and hast crowned him with glory and honour. Thou madest him to have dominion over the works of thy hands; thou has put all things under his feet."
- *Psalms 8:3-6*

10
The World is a Better Place Because of Who You Are

You are so very important to the health and wellness of the world, and I hope you know this and acknowledge it. No matter who you are, where you live on Planet Earth, what your background has been, what color your skin is, what form of worship you practice, what useful occupation you have, you are a good person and the world is better because of you. Bless yourself and every man, woman and child with whom you share your life with this realization. Bless yourself and your world with the understanding of how vital you are to the overall evolutionary process.

If you are new to these ideas and the thought of being important to the evolutionary process is too much to presently comprehend, be aware of how you interact with and, influence, your known circle of family, friends and associates. Every constructive thought you think, every uplifting feeling you have, benefits those whom you know. Beyond this, your silent influence extends to the smallest units of matter and to the places beyond the most distant galaxy. You do not think a thought or feel a feeling, however small or large, but that the universe is influenced. The electro-magnetic field in the space your body now resides is altered every time you blink an eyelid. This latter happening has already been measured by scientists, using special instruments for the purpose.

When you are happy, the world is made more happy. When you are depressed, the world reacts to that depression. When you are healthy, the world is made more healthy. When you are ill, the world is more challenged. When you are enlightened, the world is more bright. When you are not enlightened, the world continues in a routine of oppositions and inclinations to balance matters in the direction of final purpose.

I could quote a thousand or more sources to emphasize this theme. I would be but repeating what has been said so well, so many times before. No man is an island. We are all one family. The universe is one organic whole. Not a sparrow falls but that God knows. Wherever unrighteousness tends to overcome righteousness, I (God) intervene to set virtue on her seat again. It does not seem to matter who seems to say it; the intelligence behind the total life process is saying it all. Sometimes the words flow to meet our mind as though set to music. At other times the words are almost harsh in their brevity. It is always the one essence speaking and the one essence listening and responding, and the result is beauty and recognition.

Why, then, if it has all been said before, do we say it again and again? Because, as one person put it, when truth is restated, the words are made fresh and offered in a new way to the same ears or, in the same way, to new ears. And, how often we sometimes need to hear the obvious before the spark within us is kindled into a flaming fire! A few strokes of the hammer may not heat the metal sufficiently to work it, but with continued application the metal is, at last, rendered malleable so that the desired end is realized. We cannot know for sure which stroke of the hammer was most effective, when it was that shapeless form began to become a work of art. We cannot know for ourselves which word, which insight, which fleeting thought or small decision, made the difference in our lives. But, we must persist. We must continue our awakening way until completion is our experience.

There will never be another you. When you were born into the world, something unique took place. No one has ever had your thoughts before. No person has ever felt your feelings, dreamed your dreams, responded to life as you have responded. Nothing you have ever done, or will do, can ever exactly be duplicated by another. No person has ever loved as you have loved, or been loved as you have been loved.

Do you see how special you are? From the larger ocean of life, you came into expression. Your way is personal. When you awaken to your personal way, do not depart from it because your way is the way of destiny. It is good to have the acknowledgement of others; it is even better to have the inner acknowledgement of the soul which informs you that you are in the right place in life, and that all is well with you as you go about your appointed rounds.

If you had not been born into the world, the world would not be as it is, because you have made a difference. You will continue to make a difference as you unfold, expand and move in the direction of liberation of consciousness. What kind of future difference would you like to make in the world? Ask the question of yourself, and answer from the depths of your being.

What you have done is done, and what you have been in relationship to your world is what you have been. What you will do, and what you will be in relationship with your awakening world, is up to you.

I ACCEPT FULFILLMENT NOW

Be alone and meditate until you experience inner peace. Without hurry or anxiety read the following. *Affirm, know* and *feel* the *truth* about yourself. Remember, God is your companion in life's adventure. You are destined for fulfillment and total understanding. God, as you, came into manifestation to express His highest qualities and attributes.

I Accept Self-Realization Now

I know I am a specialized unit of God consciousness, endowed with all of the attributes of the Divine. I will practice needed disciplines, study the nature of consciousness, meditate regularly and surrender ego-sense in order to be consciously aware of my Larger True Self.

I Accept Mental Clarity and Creativity Now

I resolve to regulate my mental pictures, adjust my attitude, see my environment clearly and to fully cooperate with Universal Mind. I will set and achieve useful goals in harmony with the highest ideals.

I Accept Emotional Wellness Now

I will come to terms with past experiences, relationships and perceptions. I will live appropriately and wisely in the present. I will anticipate the near and distant future with serenity, knowing that God is in charge of His own world and that His grace sustains me, always.

I Accept Health and Vitality Now
I am established in health-consciousness because I know that true health and vitality extends from the soul level, through mind and into the body. I will abide by natural laws relative to nutrition, exercise, rest and freedom from stress.

I Accept Loving and Supportive Relationships Now
I know that all people are incarnations of the Divine. I will do my part to love and support others and I will expect God, through and as other people, to love and support me. In all relationships I will serve God and I will allow God to serve me.

I Accept Prosperity and True Fulfillment Now
I know that to prosper means to thrive, to flourish and to be successful in useful ways. I fill real needs. I see human hurts and heal them. I am always open to my unplanned good as God meets me at my level of need, on time and in abundance. I share my life and Life's abundance wisely and generously.

I consciously acknowledge this agreement between God and myself and inwardly pledge that I will do my utmost to abide by my commitment.

APPENDIX & NOTES

Because it seems useful to do so, the remaining pages of this book will be used to supplement preceding chapters and to make suggestions and recommendations. The journey to discovery is never completed until we rest in total awareness of the truth about ourselves as the larger field of consciousness.

It may seem that emphasis upon methods and procedures might incline one to become overly involved with technique, even self-centered. The purpose of methods and procedures is to offer a person the opportunity to experiment, to cause inner and outer change, to allow for growth and new perceptions. When disciplines and guidelines are shared it must be understood that what is recommended is that which is already natural and spontaneous for a truly conscious person. A conscious person does not have to work at being correct in actions and response. A conscious person automatically, not mechanically, acts and responds in appropriate fashion no matter the environment or the situation. One good reason for our involvement with methods and procedures is that we are often in need of change for the better. We are often in need of genuine transformation. This is because we are prone, as conditioned beings, to find a convenient level in life and remain in it. To be consciously comfortable is the ideal; to be "stuck" in a living pattern which is short of the ideal is a restriction.

While in conditioned consciousness we are inclined to be satisfied with convenience and ease. We are inclined to settle for less than full actualization of our potential because we are living without challenge and we are "getting by" and "doing fine" in comparison with the general pattern acceptable to others who are considered to be normal in today's society. I do not want you to settle for being normal, I want you to consider being *natural.* To be natural is to be conscious, fully functional and expressive of all of the qualities and characteristics of your inner potential.

Life does not have to be a struggle. How often have we exclaimed, "When will it end?", as we have felt ourselves to be almost driven to the limits of our patience? We do not have to put up with pain, suffering, confusion, limitations and the variety of miseries common to many in human consciousness. There will come that fine moment in our experience when we awaken from all that is not in harmony with freedom, total health and function in all areas of daily life. We have before us the opportunity to shorten the time of waiting. Lest any person think that change and transformation is always without inner challenge, let him read the lives of the saints or, even, the lives of most who have extended themselves beyond the level of what is considered to be normal awareness and behavior. It sometimes "hurts like hell" to make necessary changes. That's what hell is; the pain and conflict common to unenlightened consciousness. Heaven is the experience of harmony, right action, steady unfoldment and the certain experience of grace in our lives.

There is a supportive and nourishing influence pervading all of nature and when this is evident in our lives we refer to it as the activity of grace. It is at this time that we are so open to the flow that we are carried along with little effort on our part. Before this experience it seemed as though we were everlastingly working at causing effects and trying to make something happen. Which leads us to an often asked question: "How can I tell the difference between my personal will and God's will?" The answer to this question has been the subject of debate for centuries.

Appendix & Notes

In the early stages, as we quest for the ideal life experiences, we certainly make mistakes in judgement. Often, our ego drives get in the way and our impatience causes us to push too hard, even in the right direction. We may want more than we can presently handle. We may strive to create a world based upon immature speculations. We may forget that we are but waves on the ocean of cosmic consciousness and that the larger life has a plan and a purpose in which we are included. It is not up to us to have plans and purposes in which the larger life is included. This is to turn matters around and create an impossible obstacle for ourselves. To paraphrase another, "What will it gain us to acquire the whole world, yet, miss the whole point of our being here?"

This, then is a major challenge—to find our place in the larger plan and to do our duty as we are expected to do it. If it were but a matter of our getting through this present life-cycle and reaching the grave with reasonable discomfort, almost anyone could succeed. We did not begin with physical birth and we will not end with the body's end. Therefore, we are compelled to think in more far-reaching terms and references. We are compelled to think in terms and references which include our forever nature as spiritual beings. This throws new light on the subject for many.

It would be easy for me to write an inspirational book designed to motivate the reader to experience reasonable health, acceptable happiness and adequate prosperity. Even partially aware people can be taught to function in society and provide for themselves the basic requirements for pain-free living. Millions in today's world are at this level of awareness and must be educated to basic matters regarding physical, emotional and mental comfort. Since life is an organic whole, we must see to the welfare and the general good of all people. Because you are reading this book, you are not content to cope with circumstances. You are aspiring to the highest and best which is possible for you. You are responding from your innate level of awareness to dismiss, once and forever, the mistaken beliefs of limitation.

Aspiration alone, while a powerful force to accomplishment, is not sufficient. Along with aspiration there must be a conscious intention to make necessary changes and to accept awakening and unfoldment. We are in the dawning of the Age of Enlightenment and we have the force of evolution working with us and, through us. All who wisely strive now for self-actualization are more likely to be successful in their ventures. All who do their part now will make a lasting influence felt upon the fabric of planetary consciousness. Do you realize what a marvelous opportunity you now have before you? You have the opportunity to be a conscious participant in the most transformative phase of human history! Do not let the opportunity pass without giving it the best of which you are now capable.

How Do You See Your World?

In the first chapter of this book I discussed the fact that we are inclined to perceive our world through our own mental "screens" or, preconceptions. We are inclined to see only what we want to see, what we have been taught to see, or what suits our purposes at the moment. A failure, for instance, will find it almost impossible to see success patterns. A successful person, on the other hand, cannot see a reason for failure. Some people see only the good in others. A common habit is to see only that which is not good. One person may see opportunity in a situation while another would see an impossible condition. Sages of various cultures have taught that the world is an appearance and is subject to our analysis and intent. We can draw almost any conclusion when we view an external condition. We can, also, often change the condition if we want to do so. We can always change ourselves and our way of looking at life.

Appendix & Notes

A useful book for the reader to examine is *Stations of the Mind* by William Glasser, M.D. The author is well known for his earlier writings on the subject of *reality therapy,* the approach taken that we are responsible for our lives. Because of the rapid change of publishing trends, that of phasing books from hardbound editions to paperback form, unless I mention a publisher for a book which is referred to, simply contact your book dealer and ask for the title in whatever form available. It is my opinion that all of the writings of Dr. Glasser are deserving of careful attention.

Taking the Confusion Out of a Common Term

Enlightenment is said to be a goal for many on the path to personal freedom. Are there degrees of enlightenment? Of course there are, because whenever we experience insight we are, to a degree, more enlightened. Teachers in the Zen tradition stress that one is either enlightened or, if not fully so, is experiencing degrees of delusion. Let us not complicate the matter by indulging in a game of words. We have said (*Chapter Two*) that it is natural to be enlightened. When we are truly conscious, we are most natural. Insight may be experienced in a flash. Insight may also emerge as the sun brings light when it emerges over the eastern horizon. The light of the soul may gently surface, resulting in steady but constant illumination.

There are at least two possible snares on the enlightenment path. One is that we may assume that we are enlightened before we truly are and, because of our immaturity, we may barge ahead with noble cause but with ego apparent to everyone but ourselves. The other possible limitation is that we become ready for more liberated living but we cling to a shred of personality-sense and refuse to flow with the stream of evolutionary influence. We deny our own divinity by refusing to surrender the final semblance of delusion. The key is to pray for guidance and enter into a more total relationship with the larger life. In this way we cannot fail to fulfill our destiny. It can also be useful to have the support and guidance of a truly enlightened person, a guru, but this must be a matter of individual destiny. The worst possible mistake would be to go about frantically looking for a guru. The true guru is the intelligence of God and this intelligence will guide us to make the right contacts when we are open to such guidance.

Evidence of increasing enlightenment will reflect as mental clarity, emotional stability, physical health, supportive relationships and a greater degree of personal freedom to function on a day to day basis. Even when we know the principles, even when we know how to live, we may be self-limited because of fear to express, immaturity, selfishness, or an attitude of limitation. Enlightenment results in a more cosmic awareness so that we have a clear and satisfying overview of life and relationships.

The Mind/Brain Connection

The brain is the organ of the mind as we relate to the world in which we live. The mental field is not fully contained within the brain because we can still use mental abilities when we depart the body. Mystics tell us this to be so, and ordinary people who have experienced involuntary out-of-body incidents report the same thing. Because the mind is superior to the brain, and the being (the real person) is superior to the mind, the degree of intelligence with which we were born is not fixed. We can become increasingly intelligent as we become increasingly functional and aware. Do not ever allow yourself to believe that you are lacking in the capacity to be intelligent and fully functional!

As the mental field is cleared, as intelligence becomes increasingly more keen, as intuition awakens, as the soul nature becomes more influential, we find that we have access to an unbounded range of creative possibilities. As we experience freedom from inner restrictions we manifest freedom in daily affairs.

It is useful to nourish the mind with information and to provide inspiration for the soul by whatever useful means possible. Whatever you can read, see or experience that will awaken your innate potential will be helpful to you. Audio cassette tapes are an extremely useful tool to this end. Video presentations offer the extra impact and stimulation of visual input. The acquisition of data is one thing, the important part of the learning process is to put into practice the concepts learned. Make information your own by practical application. Provide success experiences for the mind and the mind will be naturally inclined to continue the creative involvement.

**Imagination and Will
Overcomes All Barriers**

We are never defeated as long as we possess the capacity to imagine, to visualize, to plan for useful change. We do not all start life with equal advantages. We do, however, have the inner ability to extend ourselves beyond all barriers. We can image possibilities and move into them. We can desire needed support and attract it. The will to succeed calls forth sleeping powers and talents. Even persons with physical handicaps can adapt, innovate and succeed beyond human expectation. The key is, never accept limitation. Do not believe those who are negative in their outlook. Go with the doers, live like the winners, prove the laws of mind and consciousness in your personal life.

Meeting with others who share your aspirations can be helpful. Perhaps a weekly study, discussion and meditation group could be formed. Many communities have groups representative of the New Thought movement which offer regular programs. These include Unity, Religious Science, Divine Science, Science of Mind and others. Many areas have yoga teachers who offer classes. Whatever we can do to assist the awakening and actualization of our powers is useful. When you find that approach, that discipline, which is most beneficial to your purposes, adhere to it while being respectful of the ways taken by others.

Do not underestimate the importance of writing your goals, your plans, your projects. This will enable you to enter into a program of change. One of the most common practices we use to avoid success is that of procrastination. Use the methods found helpful by other successful people until you reach that level of awareness which enables you to function spontaneously without guidelines and procedures.

**Return to the Source
of Power and Creativity**

A person who feels healthy may neglect health practices. Likewise, a person who feels clear and functional may neglect meditation. Be sure to maintain a regular meditation schedule even during your most creative and functional phases. This will insure that you remain open and in the flow of life. This will insure that you remain free from stress. Stress can accumulate at deeper levels when we are not aware of it. Decision making, planning of goals, relating to others, all such involvements provide a degree of challenge and the possibility of our experiencing stress in the nervous system and body. Manage stress by meditating on a regular schedule.

After meditation, be open to the power that runs the universe and feel yourself to be in partnership with it. Set your goals, work your plans and be patient when patience is required. Learn to flow with circumstances so that your timing is appropriate. Cycles of activity are present in all natural happenings. When an actualization cycle is present, unfold with it. When the cycle of rest and preparation is present, be patient and mildly anticipate the emergence of the actualization cycle. Read the chapter on meditation again to be sure you know how to meditate and to check your practice.

**Self-Love is
Self-Respect**

The basis of emotional health is self-esteem. If you really like yourself as a being, you will release conflicts and do all within your power to experience emotional wellness. How can we truly respect others if we do not respect ourselves? How can we ever feel deserving of good fortune if we do not respect ourselves? While being respectful of yourself, practice non-judgemental respect in relationship to others. This is one of the most useful procedures I can recommend and it will require close attention to the process to be successful. If we respect ourselves we will never do anything harmful or self-destructive. If we respect others, we will be able to do nothing except to love and bless them.

In chapter eight the theme centered on relationships. In many of the world's scriptures we are informed that when one is firmly established in harmlessness, when one can only love and bless others and all living things, one will never have to fear and will never experience hardship, accident or impoverishment. The reason for this is, when we are on friendly terms with the universe the universe provides for us because we are open to this influence. Whenever you have a problem in a relationship, examine your inner attitude and feelings to see if you are as loving and supportive as you should be. Much of our emotional pain is due to our selfishness. It is absolutely true that the more we give of ourselves to others, the more life provides for us. Never think that giving and supporting in any way diminishes you. Realize that life, through you, is providing for expressions of itself as other people and the planet. When we give correctly life provides us with all that is required, on time and in abundance.

Be Open to Infinite Good

That which is good is that which is in accord with being conscious, happy, healthy and fully functional. Anything which contributes to unconsciousness, misery, illness and restriction is contrary to evolutionary intention. Life is moving in the direction of fulfillment of purposes. It is easy for us to determine whether or not we are in tune with evolutionary forces by examining what our experiences are and what the future holds for us if we continue in our present trend. As we review the past few weeks, months and years, can we see evidence of unfoldment and growth? Are we becoming more wise, possessed of greater understanding, and are we more successful in fulfilling our purposes?

Do not feel guilty because you are prospering and others are not. You cannot help others if you are not living the ideal life. On the other hand, when you are fulfilled you can show others the way to fulfillment. One need not look far to observe evidence of poverty and limitation among members of the human race. It is natural for us to have compassion upon those who seem less fortunate. It is also our duty, to the degree in which we are able, to assist our brothers and sisters in the direction of awakening and self-sufficiency. To see to education, to show people how to help themselves, is one of the most useful things we can do. What we have found to be useful in our own lives will be useful to others. Remember, we share a common sameness with all who walk the face of the earth. We also share common aspirations, and we all are possessed of the same innate potential. When helping others, do not be easily discouraged if they fail to respond in a positive manner. They have their freedom of choice and they have their own lessons to learn. We do the best we can for others and then we allow life to deal with them as it knows best.

Establish a psychic connection (a soul connection) with the substance of this world and learn to make wise use of it. If we are not attached to things, if we are not repelled by things, we can be objective and intelligent in the use of things. There is a reason and a purpose for this world and there is a reason and a purpose for your being in the world. Find this reason for your being here and make the most of the opportunity. One of the most available occasions of spiritual growth is to be found right where we are.

We are not all called upon to play outwardly dramatic roles in life. What life has determined for us, what we determine with life, is our allotted role and the place of destiny. Love and bless the opportunity now before you to learn and to unfold. By being responsible for what life has given you to do now, you will prepare yourself for whatever life gives you later.

Books and Aids to Encourage Growth

For a list of my available books, audio cassettes and video programs contact the publisher. A useful supplement to *The Potential Is Within You* is my title, *How You Can Use the Technique of Creative Imagination*. For an in depth examination of the nature of consciousness and a commentary on the *Yoga Sutras*, read my book *The Teachings of the Masters of Perfection*.

The books by William Glasser, M.D. are excellent for the purpose of encouraging the reader to be self-honest, responsible and realistic in relationships and behavior. *Reality Therapy* and *Stations of the Mind* by Dr. Glasser are especially recommended. The writings of Norman Vincent Peale have served millions of people with a positive thinking message. Writings by Dr. Shuller, popular television minister, are highly motivational. Other authors whose books have stood the test of time are Emmet Fox, Joel S. Goldsmith, Neville, Ernest Holmes, Napoleon Hill, Clement Stone and Robert Collier. A classic which should not be overlooked is Paramahansa Yogananda's *Autobiography of a Yogi*. Useful magazines are *Truth Journal* (of which I am Editor), *Unity* magazine, *Science of Mind, Guideposts* and *Success Unlimited.*

A most useful title to have is *Diet & Nutrition* by Rudolph Ballentine, M.D., published by the Himalayan International Institute, Honesdale, Pennslyvania. An endless source of inspiration and delight is *Bartlett's Familiar Quotations.* A provocative book to read is *The Tao of Physics* by Fritjof Capra, published by Shamballa Publications. Useful for the purpose of expanding awareness are books and articles on Einstein's theory of relativity and any material dealing with science and the nature of man and the universe.

Note: If you are one who works with people to educate and motivate, you may want to share copies of *The Potential Is Within You* with others. The publisher allows attractive discounts for this purpose. Write CSA Press, Post Office Box 7, Lakemont, Georgia 30552 and request information.